Contents

D0189305

Introduction

There are plenty of GCSE English textbooks on the market, so what makes this one any different?

First, this textbook is written by three highly experienced examiners who have examined both Paper 1 and Paper 2 at senior levels. We have decades of examining and teaching experience between us, experience we have pooled in our endeavour to make sure this is not only an interesting and engaging read but, most importantly, a foundation for exam success.

Second, the main reason this project was suggested was to provide a different way of approaching GCSE English by focusing on the Assessment Objectives upon which the AQA GCSE English course is based.

Third, the integral use of examiner comments on sample student work gives you an unprecedented view into the mind of an examiner. This will not only help you to make sense of the world of examining and assessment, but allow you to assess yourself (known as Assessment for Learning in modern educational parlance) and to see the clear links between one grade and the next.

Finally, this book is different from other textbooks in terms of its structure. Its first two sections cover the portable skills of reading and writing. For this reason, although this is mainly a GCSE English textbook, we realised that here was an opportunity to reinforce the links between the reading and writing Assessment Objectives, wherever they may be assessed. You must find evidence to back up your explanations in coursework, Paper 1, Paper 2 and Literature, so it makes sense to focus on the portable skill rather than the content. This explains the inclusion of a chapter that focuses on the broad skills needed to respond to the skills in literature rather than discussing each of the different poems and novels in turn. The third section of the book includes practice examinations that show you the examining process through the eyes of an examiner, with plenty of feedback and hints on how to improve your grades. The key here is to approach the exams with the Assessment Objectives firmly in mind.

So, get started and boost your grade by taking the advice of the experts!

John Nield
Paul Pascoe
Martin Walker

Acknowledgements

We are grateful for copyright permission from the following groups:
David Higham Associates Ltd for 'Timothy Winters'; Anne Nichols and John Richardson for 'Reveal your super self!'; Penguin Books Ltd for 'One Wednesday Afternoon'; Robert Fox's Estate for 'A Fable'; Royal Mail Film Archive for 'Night Mail'; A. P. Watt Ltd on behalf of the Literary Executors of the Estate of H. G. Wells for *The War of the Worlds*.

Extracts are reproduced from the following books:
Bryson, Bill (1995) *Notes on a Small Island*, Black Swan.
Causley, Charles (1957) 'Timothy Winters', *Union Street*.
Fox, Robert (1986) 'A Fable', from Shapard, R. and Thomas, J. (eds) *Sudden Fiction: American Short Stories*, Penguin.
Hemingway, Ernest (1994) *The Old Man and the Sea*, Arrow.
Jaffrey, Madhur (1985) *A Taste of India*, Pavilion.
Le Carré, John (1999) *The Looking Glass War*, Sceptre.
Levy, Andrea (1999) *The Fruit of the Lemon*, Headline.
Theroux, Paul (1975) *The Great Railway Bazaar*, Penguin.
Wells, H. G. (1898) *The War of the Worlds*, A. P. Watt.

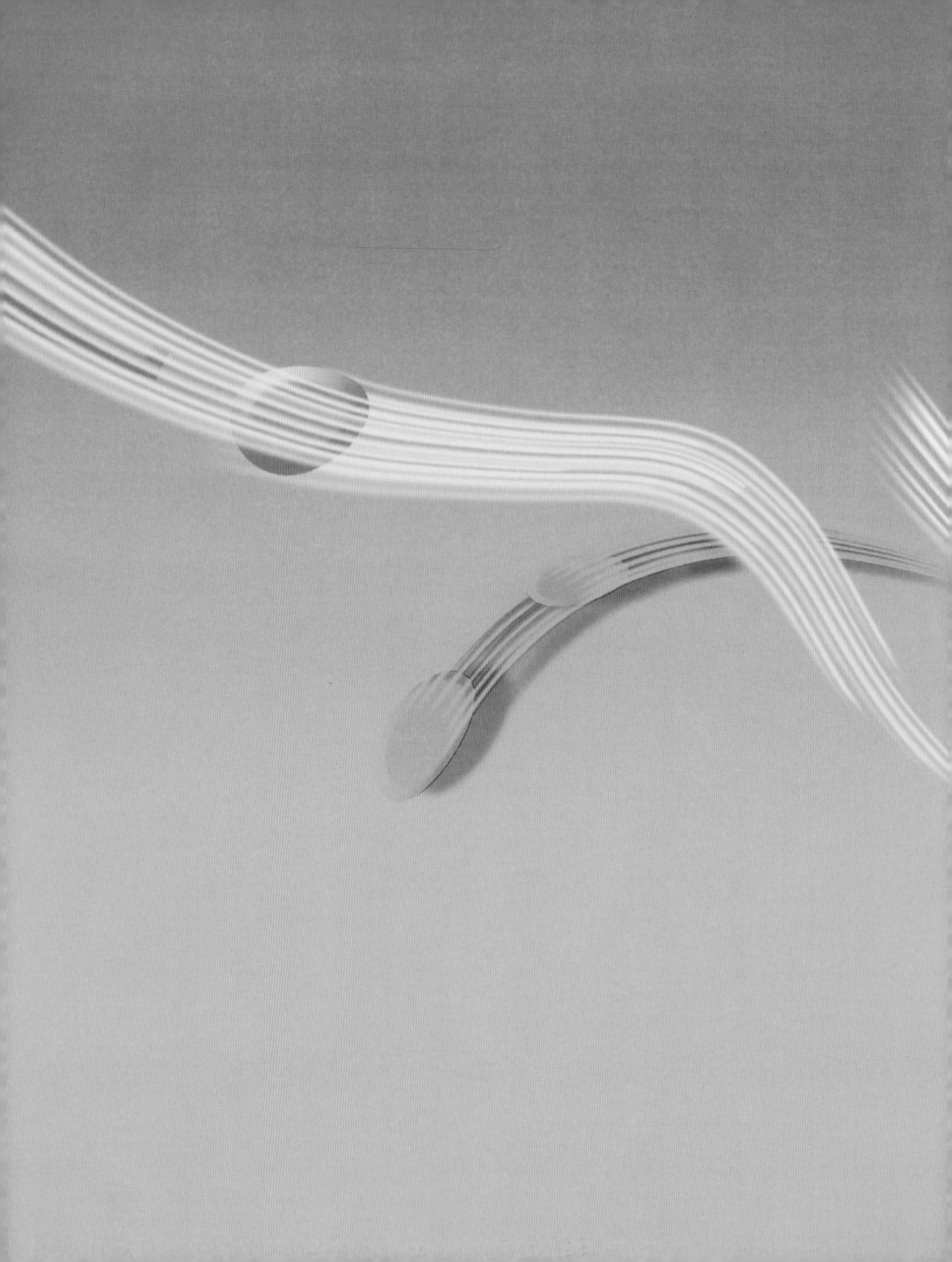

Reading

Assessment Objectives for reading

Most people can read. We do it all the time and it certainly seems easier than writing. So why does reading amount to 40% of the marks for GCSE English? The answer is found in what examiners are required to assess.

Under the topic of reading you are required to show that you can read with insight, distinguish between fact and fiction, follow an argument, select material from different sources and comment on language. In other words, there is much more to reading than simply casting your eyes over pages of print. In fact, unless an examiner could plug into your brain and find out your thoughts directly, the only way your reading can be tested is through your writing. To read successfully for the examination, you must learn how to **write** about what you read.

What are you required to read? First, you must read some literature, regardless of whether or not you are entering the English Literature examination. Some is set for coursework under the guidance of your teacher, but you also need to study poetry from different cultures for the written examination. Second, you have to study some non-fiction, including media texts, for the written examination.

Your reading will be assessed against the following five **Assessment Objectives (AOs)**:

AO2(i)	Read with insight and engagement, making appropriate references to texts and developing and sustaining interpretations of them.
AO2(ii)	Distinguish between fact and opinion and evaluate how information is presented.
AO2(iii)	Follow an argument, identifying implications and recognising inconsistencies.
AO2(iv)	Select material appropriate to your purpose, collate material from different sources, and make cross-references.
AO2(v)	Understand and evaluate how writers use linguistic, structural and presentational devices to achieve their effects, and comment on ways language varies and changes.

Assessment Objective	Paper 1	Paper 2	Coursework task 1 (Shakespeare)	Coursework task 2 (prose study)
2(i)	✓	✓	✓	✓
2(ii)	✓			
2(iii)	✓			
2(iv)	✓	✓	✓	✓
2(v)	✓	✓	✓	✓

As the grid above shows, some Assessment Objectives are more important than others because they are tested in all four reading tasks. One of these is AO2(i).

AO2(i)

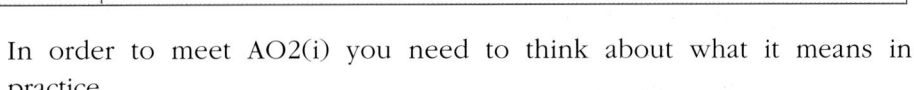

Read with insight and engagement, making appropriate references to texts and developing and sustaining interpretations of them

Key words	What the key words mean
read with insight and engagement	You can find out about a text and look beyond its word-for-word meaning. You can look at the text from different angles and show an interest in the writing.
appropriate references	You can choose the relevant parts of a text to support your comments.
developing and sustaining interpretations	You can develop a series of connected comments about a whole text and show that a text can have wider meanings.

In order to meet AO2(i) you need to think about what it means in practice.

❊ You must understand the basic **content** — what the words and sentences mean literally. For example, if your teacher announced, 'You are the most supremely perspicacious group of cognoscenti I have ever encountered', you would obviously need to know the meaning of 'perspicacious' and 'cognoscenti' before you could work out what is being said.

❊ You must be able to grasp the overall **subject** of the words. In the example in the point above, the subject of the teacher's words is the students' ability.

❊ You must interpret, or 'read between the lines', and understand the real **meaning** of the words. At first you may be flattered to discover that perspicacious means 'clear-sighted' and cognoscenti means 'knowledgeable

people'. But when you take into account that the teacher is returning some poor homework, you will realise that he/she is being sarcastic and intends the exact opposite of the words' literal meaning. Of course, a clue to the teacher's intention would be revealed in the tone of voice and gestures used. But even when we are dealing purely with the written word, we must always look beyond the simple, basic meaning.

> **Remember:** when you are reading, you must decide **what** has happened, **how** it happened and **why** it happened.

To find out the content, subject and meaning, you must think like a detective. You need to look at the **evidence**, search for **clues** and come to some **conclusions**. Look at the two short pieces of text below. Both passages are almost exactly the same length and provide information about Corsica.

Text 1

Island in the Mediterranean Sea immediately north of Sardinia, from which it is separated by the Strait of Bonifacio; a department of France. Area 8,700 km². Pop. 269,831. Prefecture Ajaccio. The interior is mountainous (with plains only along the east coast), rising to 8,891 ft in Monte Cinto. The rocky west coast has many headlands and gulfs. Over the lower mountain slopes is spread a tangled undergrowth of shrubs (Fr. maquis, Italian macchid) which used to provide cover for bandits. Farming primitive. Sheep and goats raised in large numbers. Produces olives, vines, citrus fruits, chestnuts. Growing tourist industry. The seaports Ajaccio and Bastia are the largest towns. Exports olive oil, wine, fruits etc.

Text 2

Corsica is the third largest island in the Mediterranean Sea. It sits 170 km south of France, to which it belongs, and 83 km west of Italy. Its 8,700 km² of land offer striking contrasts and a wealth of natural wonders to explore. The land itself offers much to be proud of. Nature has bestowed the gift of amazing geographical variety here. With 1,000 km of coastline, there are beaches of fine golden sand, rocky bays where fishing villages cling to sheltered coves, and sheer cliffs dropping dramatically into the azure water below. Inland a spine of vertiginous granite peaks climb to 8,891 ft, giving Corsica the nickname 'mountain in the sea'.

Task

1 In what ways are the two passages similar in the kind of basic information they provide?

2 In what ways does the second passage do more than the first?

3 From what kinds of book do you think the passages are taken and why?

Now look at a different kind of text and see what you can find out about it. In the following passage a German woman who has moved to the Ukraine describes some of her experiences of television in that country.

Where I live, the advert breaks in programmes are so long I once walked away from the TV, had a shower, washed my hair, made a cup of tea and still made it back to the couch before the show started again. Welcome to commercial breaks, Ukraine-style.¹

It's been exceedingly difficult for me not to judge Ukrainian culture by its advertising. If nothing else, I think it reflects the culture's stage of development in regard to gender equality. For example, I have yet to see a single advert where a man does any kind of domestic activity.²

There's one commercial for a stove where a husband in a suit, complete with briefcase, arrives home and says the classic line: 'Honey, I'm home.' His small son hurls himself at his father's legs and shouts, 'Papa!' The trophy wife in a frilly pinny looks on fondly.³

With a game-show flourish of her hand over the stove, she proudly lists the 12 things she cooked for dinner that night. The husband shakes his head in disbelief and says, 'Wow.' The whole thing ends with the three of them gathered around the amazing appliance.⁴

Task

What tone of voice do you think the person writing would be using if she were telling you this out loud?

Beer commercials are more reminiscent of early 80s advertising. They consist mostly of men on fishing or camping trips, doing manly things that are rewarded with a cold beer.[5]

I just love it at the end when they take a long swig, smack their chops in satisfaction and inevitably wipe their mouths on the back of their hands. Classic.[6]

I've never seen so many adverts for toothpaste, shampoo, fridges and, of course, vodka.[7]

Once again, we see a middle-aged wifey tidying in the kitchen, with her frilled apron and 50s-style hair. From another room her husband shouts imperiously: 'Coffee!' Frowning slightly at the tone, she nevertheless begins preparations for making coffee.

'Vodka!' yells her husband. Alarmed now, she scurries around the kitchen looking for vodka and a glass. Then the husband shouts another order, whereupon she frantically starts making something to eat. 'Angelina Jolie!' screams the voice from the other room. This time he's gone too far. She slams down the knife she was using and marches into the living room to investigate. On stepping into the room, the husband punches the air in triumph as he answers yet another question correctly from the game show on TV. Wifey plops down next to him on the sofa heaving a big sigh of relief. She then laughs at herself for ever having doubted him. I could honestly vomit every time I see this ad.[8]

Let's look at what is really happening in the passage. First, what does the woman tell us literally? This can be summarised by paragraph:

Paragraph **1**	The adverts are extremely long.
Paragraph **2**	One can judge a country's attitudes and culture through its advertisements. No men appear in adverts doing domestic chores.
Paragraphs **3** and **4**	A particular advert is described.
Paragraph **5**	Beer adverts are described.
Paragraph **6**	She loves the way the beer adverts end.
Paragraph **7**	She lists the kinds of product that appear frequently.
Paragraph **8**	Another advert is described and the author says she almost vomits when she sees it.

Look at the section of this book on fact and opinion (see pages 10–17).

All of the above is true, and if you simply wanted to know the content of Ukrainian advertisements it would be sufficient. However, the writer is not just telling us what appears in the advertisements — she is giving us her opinion of them.

Task

1 Answer each of the questions below.

(a) '…*commercial breaks, Ukrainian-style.*' What does 'style' suggest here?

(b) '…*gender equality.*' What has this to do with the writer's viewpoint?

(c) '…*(no advertisement) where a man does any kind of domestic activity.*' What is this evidence of?

(d) '…*classic line: "Honey, I'm home."* ' What is meant by 'classic' here and what does 'honey' suggest?

(e) '…*frilly pinny…*' What picture does this call up?

(f) '…*proudly lists the 12 things…*' Why proudly?

(g) '*Wow.*' Where have you heard that word before?

(h) '*I just love it…*' What does the writer mean: does she really love the advertisements?

(i) '…*husband punches the air in triumph…*' What sort of man does that?

(j) '*Wifey…*' What's the difference between 'wifey' and 'wife'?

(k) '*I could honestly vomit…*' Why?

2 Consider the details the author uses in her account and show how they suggest what she thinks of advertisements on Ukrainian television.

So far we have considered **non-fictional** texts, but the reading of **literary** texts is a major part of your assessment. The procedure is basically the same: you must look beyond the literal information for clues as to what the author is really saying. The difference is that plays, novels and poems often do many things at once. Literary texts are much more open to different **interpretations** than non-literary texts, so you need to have your wits about you.

Here is the opening of a short story.

Excitement boiled in the woman and overflowed in an almost incoherent torrent of words in which the gatekeeper's puny inquiry bobbed for a second, unheeded, and was lost.

'An accident, y'say?' he asked again as the woman caught at her breath. 'Jack Lister?'

Her vigorous nod set heavy flesh trembling on cheeks and chin. 'His wife…I'm his mother. They've taken her to hospital.'

'Just a minute, then.' The gatekeeper went into the gatehouse and the woman watched him through the dusty side-window as he lifted the receiver of the telephone and spoke to someone inside the low sprawl of factory buildings. In a few minutes he came out again. 'He'll be out in a minute,' he said. He eased the peak of his

uniform cap, then clasped his hands behind his back and rocked backwards and forwards, almost imperceptibly, on toes and heels as he looked down at the woman.

She said, 'Thank you,' repeating the words absently a moment later. Then suddenly, as though a tap had been turned on inside her, the gush of words started again. The gatekeeper listened placidly until she touched on the nature of the accident, when his face screwed itself into a grimace.

'Ooh, that's nasty,' he said. 'That's nasty.'

At first when the foreman spoke to him the man did not appear to understand. 'Somebody wanting me?' he said, knitting his eyebrows in perplexity.

'Aye, up at the gate. There's been a bit o' trouble or summat. I should go up an' see what's doin', if I were you.'

His mother hurried to meet him as he came out of the building into the yard, pulling on his jacket as he walked.

'It's Sylvia, Jack,' she blurted. 'She's had an accident.'

He stopped and stared at her, seeming to be wrested from his troubled absorption by her words and the sight of her, hatless and with the flowered apron visible under the unbuttoned coat. He gripped her by the upper arm, the flesh soft and yielding under his fingers. 'What's she done?' he said. 'What's happened?'

'They came to tell me, Jack. They've taken her to the infirmary. It's her hair — she's had her hair fast in a machine.'

'Oh! God,' he said.

She ran clumsily alongside him as he started for the gate. 'All that hair, Jack… She wouldn't have it cut short an' sensible. An' I bet she never even wore it fastened up like other women. She never should ha' gone out to work again anyway, but she wanted too much brass for lipstick an' donnin' up in fancy clothes… Your wage wouldn't do for her. Any decent woman would ha' been content to stop at home an' look after her bairn… I told her it wasn't right, an' she knew you didn't like it… It's a judgement on her, that's what it is…a judgement.'

Stan Barstow, 'One Wednesday Afternoon', Black Swan, 1986.

> **Do not** simpy retell the story and then stop.

The basic situation in this extract is simple. Jack's mother has come to his place of work to inform him that his wife, Sylvia, has had an accident in which her hair became entangled in a machine. They set off together for the hospital. You must understand this in order to make any sense of the story. If you do no more than this, however, you will probably get no further than Grade F.

Even in these opening paragraphs we learn more about Jack's mother and her relationship with her son and daughter-in-law than about the accident itself. Look at the highlighted words, which provide clues. Note that some of them have nothing directly to do with what is said. Try to think yourself into the situation and picture it in your mind. This is what is meant by the term '**engagement**'.

Task

1 Think about the character Jack in the above extract. He is not described directly but there are clues about him from his behaviour. Choose the actor from the four pictured below who you think would be most suitable to play Jack. Explain your choice.

Alun Armstrong   Leonardo DiCaprio   Christopher Biggins   Harrison Ford

2 Why is Jack so excited?

3 What does the way the mother speaks suggest about her feelings and attitudes?

We know that authors use their imaginations but readers have to as well. Here is a very short story. The outline is simple and easy to follow but something strange is going on.

She was standing by the river looking at the stepping stones and remembering each one. There was the round unsteady stone, the pointed one, the flat one in the middle — the safe stone where you could stand and look around. The next wasn't so safe, for when the river was full the water flowed over it and even when it showed dry it was slippery. But after that it was easy and soon she was standing on the other side.

The road was much wider than it used to be but the work had been done carelessly. The felled trees had not been cleared away and the bushes looked trampled. Yet it was the same road and she walked along feeling extraordinarily happy.

It was a fine day, a blue day. The only thing was that the sky had a glassy look that she didn't remember. That was the only word she could think of. Glassy. She turned the corner, saw that what had been the old pavé had been taken up, and there too the road was much wider, but it had the same unfinished look.

She came to the worn stone steps that led up to the house and her heart began to beat. The screw pine was gone, so was the mock summer house called the ajoupa, but the clove tree was still there and at the top of the steps the rough lawn stretched away, just as she remembered it. She stopped and looked towards the house that had been added to and painted white. It was strange to see a car standing in front of it.

There were two children under the big mango tree, a boy and a little girl, and she waved to them and called 'Hello' but they didn't answer her or turn their heads. Very

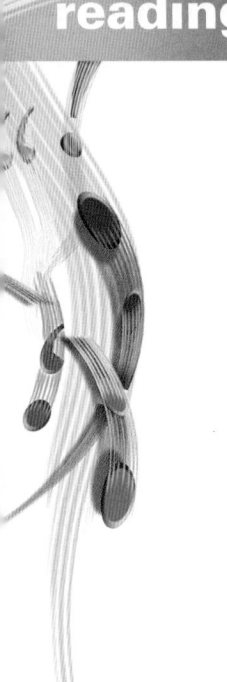

fair children, as Europeans born in the West Indies so often are: as if the white blood is asserting itself against all odds.

The grass was yellow in the hot sunlight as she walked towards them. When she was quite close she called again, shyly: 'Hello'. Then, 'I used to live here once,' she said.

Still they didn't answer. When she said for the third time 'Hello' she was quite near them. Her arms went out instinctively with the longing to touch them.

It was the boy who turned. His grey eyes looked straight into hers. His expression didn't change. He said, 'Hasn't it gone cold all of a sudden. D'you notice? Let's go in.' 'Yes let's', said the girl.

Her arms fell to her sides as she watched them running across the grass to the house. That was the first time she knew.

Jean Rhys, 'I Used to Live Here Once', from *Best West Indian Stories*, Nelson Caribbean, 1968.

Task

1 What is it that the narrator knew for the first time?

2 Explain **how** you know. What are the clues?

3 What do you think the writer is trying to express about her past?

AO2(ii)

Distinguish between fact and opinion and evaluate how information is presented

Key words	What the key words mean
distinguish between fact and opinion	You are able to identify facts and opinions and explain how they are different.
evaluate how information is presented	You can compare and contrast the different ways in which information is presented on the page

Distinguish between fact and opinion

* A **fact** is something that can be proved.
* An **opinion** is a personal view or belief that cannot be proved.

Sometimes, however, it can be difficult to tell the difference between the two because writers might:

* disguise opinion as though it is fact
* express an opinion that uses conveniently chosen facts to support it

Task

Read the following passage, which is taken from a regional leaflet on road safety, and identify the facts and opinions.

Deaths and serious injuries on our roads bring misery to thousands, including the relatives and friends of the dead and injured. Over the past three years, on average, 74 people have been killed each year, 608 seriously injured and a further 3,630 slightly injured as a result of speed-related road collisions. Most of us know someone who has been killed or seriously injured on the roads, if not as a driver or a motor-bike rider then as a cyclist or pedestrian. Many of these deaths and injuries are avoidable.

'Who? What? Why?', a leaflet published by the Safety Camera Partnership in West Mercia.

Task

Explain how each of the following could be both facts and opinions:

* Arsenal are the best!
* Girls are better than boys.
* Boys are better than girls.
* The USA is the richest country in the world.
* Rain is bad.

You might find the following example useful:

Arsenal have been arguably the best football team over recent years because of the number of cups they have won. However, it could also be argued that they have never won any cups in Europe.

Of course, people can use spurious (silly and pointless) 'facts' that are not really facts at all. It is good to be suspicious of arguments that seem to be clearly put forward.

Read the following passage from the film *Monty Python and the Holy Grail* (1975).

Crowd: A witch! A witch! A witch! We've found a witch! Burn her! Burn her! Burn her! We've found a witch! We've found a witch! A witch! A witch! A witch!

Villager 1: We have found a witch. May we burn her?

Crowd: Burn her! Burn! Burn her! Burn her!

Bedevere: How do you know she is a witch?

Villager 2: She looks like one.

Bedevere: Quiet! Quiet! Quiet! Quiet! There are ways of telling whether she is a witch.

Villager 1: Are there? What are they?

Crowd: Tell us! Tell us!...

Bedevere: Tell me. What do you do with witches?

Crowd: Burn! Burn them up! Burn!...

Bedevere: And what do you burn apart from witches?

Villager 1: More witches!

Villager 3: Shh!

Villager 2: Wood!

Bedevere: So, why do witches burn?

[pause]

Python Pictures/EMI/The Kobal Collection

Villager 3: B—...'cause they're made of...wood?

Bedevere: Good! Heh heh.

Crowd: Oh, yeah. Oh.

Bedevere: So, how do we tell whether she is made of wood?

Villager 1: Build a bridge out of her.

Bedevere: Ah, but can you not also make bridges out of stone?

Villager 1: Oh, yeah.

Bedevere: Does wood sink in water?

Villager 1: No. No.

Villager 2: No, it floats! It floats!

Villager 1: Throw her into the pond!

Crowd: The pond! Throw her into the pond!

Bedevere: What also floats in water?

Arthur: A duck!

Crowd: Oooh.

Bedevere: Exactly. So, logically...

Villager 1: If...she...weighs...the same as a duck,...she's made of wood.

Bedevere: And therefore?

Villager 2: A witch!

This is clearly full of silly arguments. No one today would believe such supposed facts — or would they?

The British Medical Association (BMA) called for the fashion industry and television to stop focusing on 'abnormally thin' celebrities such as Kate Moss, Callista Flockhart — the star of Ally McBeal, and Victoria Beckham, and for the Government to set targets for tackling the disease, anorexia nervosa. The disease affects about 2% of young women and kills a fifth of sufferers.

The Times (31 May 2000).

Task

Read the extract from *The Times* and identify the facts.

This might have seemed like a simple exercise. But the trouble with the claims made in the article is that the numbers don't make sense. The idea that anorexia affects 2% of young women and kills a fifth of sufferers is ridiculous. There are 3.5 million British women between the ages of 15 and 25. If 2% of them suffer from anorexia nervosa, that is 70,000. If a fifth die from it, we should expect 14,000 young women to die from anorexia each year. In 1999 the total number of deaths in women from this age group, from all causes, including anorexia, was 855. Can anorexia really kill 16 times more young women than even die?

Where is this assessed?

Telling the difference between fact and opinion is only assessed under exam conditions on Paper 1.

How is this assessed?

The questions tend to be different on the two tiers. On the Foundation Tier, candidates will be asked to locate, then comment on, the uses of facts and opinions. On the Higher Tier, candidates may be asked to compare how two writers have used facts and opinions in two different texts.

The following is a guide to how examiners decide the grade an answer merits:

Grade A	provides a clear, evaluative and structured judgement about the uses of facts and opinions
Grade C	clearly identifies, understands and comments on the uses of facts and opinions in a structured way
Grade F	provides a general comment on the uses of facts and the uses of opinions and attempts to identify them

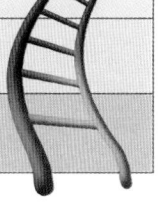

You should use the format **Point (P), Example (E), Explain (E)** to answer the questions (see pages 29–31).

 **How can you improve your answers?**

To improve your performance you have to:
* answer the question you have been given
* use the material to explain and support a point
* develop and sustain a response

Task A

Read the advertisement for girls' football boots, then answer the following questions:

1 Identify one fact and one opinion from the advert and write them down.

2 Explain how the writer uses this fact and this opinion.

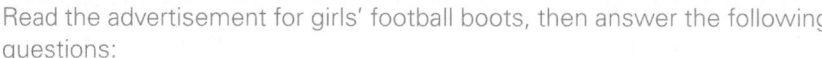

Bury it like Becca!
These boots are made for scoring

Delillo® boots have long been associated with the best in women's soccer. Now we've developed the ultimate boot with you in mind.

The obvious choice of internationals on both sides of the Atlantic, *Delillo®* boots are made for the discerning woman footballer:

✓ soft-touch kangaroo leather gives you the sort of control you want

✓ full-leather fold-over tongue gives you the comfort you need

✓ 8 removable studs give you the sort of grip you demand

Here are some views from top players:

'I was unconvinced until I scored that equaliser in last year's final. They are a brilliant boot with plenty of grip and colour that I like.'   Trudy Ulthorp

'I've buried hundreds of goals in my career, but these allow me to bury more balls in the back of the net than ever.'   Becca Gamble, England Captain

So, if you want to bury them like Becca, get down to your local sports shop where you will receive a personalised fitting and advice on after-care. After all, if boots are worth buying, they're worth looking after.

Delillo®
a lifetime of sport

Task B

Complete the same questions for the Delillo B-line Series 2006 advertisement.

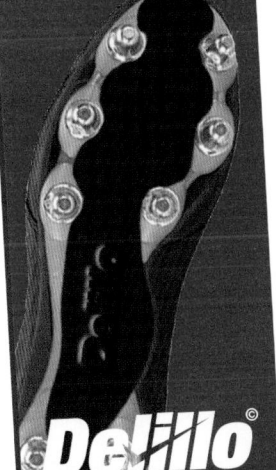

Delillo B-line Series 2006

As worn by the Everton under-16 squad

Winners of the under-16 Charity Shield 2004/05

Are your boots past their best? Are they an embarrassment in the changing room? Then make a beeline for your nearest stockist and buy a pair of Delillo B-line boots.

Delillo B-line Series is available in sizes 5–11 (inc. ½ sizes), 12 and 13. For young players who want a responsive boot with a sleek, sock-like fit. The boot has a Struction outer covering for excellent grip on all types of natural surfaces and comes in two exciting new colours.

Our price only **£28·99**
(ref. DEL1220)

Delillo ©

Task C

Compare how the two advertisements use facts and opinions. In what ways are they similar and in what ways do they differ?

Examples of student performance

Task A

Question 1 is a typical Foundation Tier question in that it really only tests lower-level reading skills. Therefore the answer will simply **identify**. The second question actually asks for an explanation. This is the sort of skill, if you can prove clearly that you have it, which will give you a mark on the Higher Tier.

Student answer

1 A fact is that they have eight removable studs. An opinion is that Delillo has 'long been associated with the best in women's soccer'.

2 I know the first one is a fact because you can prove it by counting the number of studs. The second one is an opinion because there is no way of knowing if it is true or not.

Examiner's comment

The candidate answers the first question because facts tend to lurk close to numbers, and opinions cannot be proved. How do we know that Delillo has this sort of historical link? However, this candidate is not answering the second question. He/she is explaining *why* each is a fact or opinion rather than explaining *how* they are used.

Task B

Student answer

This advertisement for Delillo B-line Series football boots uses the fact that they were worn by the under-16 Charity Shield winning Everton side because some people will be impressed if this side wore them. It is, however, an opinion that the two new colours are 'exciting'. The writers of this advert use these words because they know that purchasers are impressed by positive sounding adjectives like 'new' and 'exciting'.

Examiner's comment

This student clearly answers question 2, by explaining why she thinks her choices of fact and opinion have been used. His/her reasons are valid, so this would gain a mark in the C band.

Task C

Student answer

The two advertisements use facts for very similar reasons: they both use them to give positive views of the boots they are selling and to give information. The first advert quotes three bulleted facts which are intermingled with opinions. These facts are used in the same way as the second advert uses facts about materials and price, to inform the reader.

Similarly, because they are both promotional adverts, the writers use opinions for broadly similar reasons. They use adjectives to give biased and opinionated views about their products. In the first advert words like 'ultimate', 'obvious' and 'discerning' are used, while the second advert uses similarly biased adjectives, such as 'excellent' and 'exciting' in order to influence the reader's choice.

Examiner's comment

This is the best of the three responses for several reasons:

✳ The student has clearly answered the question by using the highlighted comparison and structuring words.

✳ There is some detail in this answer.

✳ Short quotations are embedded in the answer.

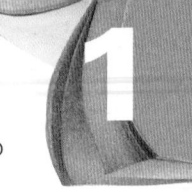

* The student uses sophisticated vocabulary, such as 'biased', which helps to conceptualise the response.

The skills it shows mean that this answer would gain a mark in the A/A* band.

Evaluate how information is presented

To **evaluate** means to appraise, judge, assess, rate, size up, value and weigh up. In practice, evaluating for Paper 1 means that you have to look at aspects of **presentation** used in newspapers, advertisements, leaflets, posters etc. You need to consider:

* what presentational devices are used
* how these presentational devices affect the reader

Typical presentational devices include:

* headlines
* illustrations
* fonts
* italics
* bullets

* sub-headings
* colour
* bold
* columns
* word art

Where is this assessed?

Again, this is only assessed under examination conditions in Paper 1, although you may use some reading skills when completing the written coursework on media. AO2(ii) is usually assessed alongside AO2(v), but it is worth looking at now and having another look later on, because it is worth so many marks.

The important word in this part of the Assessment Objective is 'evaluate', because it points to a higher-order reading skill. The ability or not to evaluate, or to assess the value of, one or more texts distinguishes between B- and C-grade responses. At Grade B there will be evidence of some clear evaluation, or weighing up the value of how well information is presented.

How is this assessed?

Grade A	a detailed answer with clear evidence that the candidate has taken the whole passage into consideration and has selected precise details in order to support comments
Grade C	a clear attempt at the question with some material selected to support comments
Grade F	an attempt to engage with the task, with simple paraphrasing, or retelling the story

How can you improve your answers?

There are many opportunities for you to become familiar with the kind of material that you will be asked to read in English Paper 1 Section A. The more you know about such material *before* you go into the examination, the better you are likely to perform on the day. These opportunities include times when you are:

* reading a variety of media for your written media coursework
* evaluating how a range of leaflets on the same subject are presented, e.g. health issues, local transport
* evaluating a range of newspaper front pages, advertisements, fliers, television adverts, logos, cartoons, film openings, CD covers, soap operas etc.
* looking at a range of past papers and focusing on the presentation questions, e.g. the teaching advert in 2002, the cycling leaflet in 2001

Now read the front page of the *Daily Express* covering the aftermath of the tsunami in Indonesia and Thailand.

Task

Evaluate how well the information is presented on the front page of the *Daily Express*.

Masthead: the title block or logo that identifies the paper.

Kicker: a story designed to stand out.

Exclusive: a story or article only covered by the paper.

Picture: an image linked with a story.

Caption: typed text under photographs which explain the image.

Headline: the main statement, usually with the biggest font size, which describes the main story.

Standfirst: the introductory paragraph before the start of the feature. (See right)

The country's worst fears were realised yesterday as the number of Britons dead in the tsunami tragedy rose to 200. The figure is one of the biggest British death tolls in a natural catastrophe and is expected to rise, with the total toll among all nations estimated at 165,000. News of the appalling loss of life came as Tony Blair faced a public backlash for failing to recognise the scale of a disaster that has moved the world.

Examples of student performance

Here are three attempts at this task, each followed by the views of an examiner.

Student answer 1

There are three main parts to this front page of the *Daily Express*. The first thing you notice is the headline and this tells you that 200 British people have died in the tsunami. It is very big and next to it is a picture of a mother who sacrificed her life to save the life of her daughter. The photograph is very colourful and looks like a family snap. The other main part of this front page is the part at the top of the page which has nothing to do with the main story, but is advertising a free personal horoscope feature with Justin Toper. This aims to tell you what's in store over the next year.

Examiner's comment

This is an attempt at the question, but it is really a paraphrase, or retelling, of the 'stories' on the front page. The candidate notices that the photograph looks like a family snap but does not make any comment about why this might be. The answer would gain a Grade E/F, because the candidate is tending only to identify.

Student answer 2

I am going to look at how well the front page of this edition of the *Daily Express* is presented and I am going to evaluate how well done it is. First, it is a particularly tragic front page and they have chosen to make the headline the most notable feature. It is in very large letters, or font, and it certainly attracts your attention. I would say that this is a successful presentational device. The top section of the page advertising your 'personal horoscope' seems rather out of place on such a front page, but it is successful in gaining the reader's interest because it is so colourful. I do not think that the photograph of the astrologer helps. Finally, there is a photograph of a victim of the tsunami and the daughter whose life she saved. This is a colourful photograph which certainly gains the reader's attention and makes the reader want to find out more about this particular story.

Examiner's comment

Once again, this is a perfect illustration of a performance at a particular grade — this time a Grade C. The student clearly attempts to evaluate three aspects of how well the front page of the newspaper is presented. He makes a point (P), finds a relevant example (E) and gives an explanation (E). This shows that the material has been selected and arranged to fit the answer.

The first sentence is pointless, however, because it simply states the obvious by repeating the words of the task.

Student answer 3

In my opinion, this front page of a middle-of-the-road tabloid newspaper is a mess. It is very bitty and is almost disrespectful towards the victims of the tsunami wave. It might be successful in fulfilling its primary role — to sell more copies of the *Daily Express* — but it is a dog's dinner of presentational devices that do not complement each other.

First, the most successful aspect of the front page is the headline, which clearly attracts the reader's attention by its font and monumental size. There is only room for a standfirst, so the reader has to buy the paper in order to read the copy linked with the headline. This is a successful presentational device.

Second, the photograph of the 'Brave mum and her daughter' is very poor quality and reflects the desperate nature of much of the coverage of this tragic event. This is obviously a family digital photograph and is almost disrespectful towards the family in its lack of professionalism. We understand the reason why the photo is a digital family snap, but we do not have to condone the inclusion of second-rate images on the front page of a national newspaper.

Finally, we come to the kicker at the top of the page. It is garishly coloured in primary colours and draws attention to 'Britain's favourite astrologer'. The presentation of this 'free' feature is very overbearing and would tend to stop discerning readers from wanting to buy this newspaper with its unflattering photograph and the headline which seems to work against the main headline on the page and to detract from its effect.

I think the presentation of this page is very poor. It fulfils its role of trying to sell more copies of the newspaper, but it fails to present a front page which directs the reader to the stories that really matter in the paper.

Examiner's comment

This answer would gain top marks, not because it is longer but because it shows that the student has actually absorbed the material and shaped it to fit the particular question. Notice that, like the Grade F candidate, this student spotted the family photograph, but instead of simply describing it she has commented on **how** the newspaper uses it. Here are the actual skills for Grade A listed in the mark scheme:

* clear and detailed understanding of what the question is asking
* careful and logical argument, backed up with examples
* material fully absorbed and shaped for purpose
* sophisticated and convincing use of technical terminology to describe media concepts

A word about the final bullet point — this is not just a matter of knowing the terminology, but being able to use it convincingly and in a way that is helpful, as a

sort of shorthand. Use of the word 'kicker' is not showing off — it is a recognised term in journalism and helps the student because it shows she knows such things exist and why they are used.

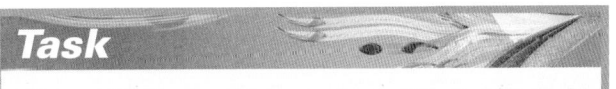

Task

What skills do you think are demonstrated by each of the highlighted examples in the final answer?

Remember: all candidates should be able to spot material; the better ones are able to evaluate it.

AO2(iii)

Follow an argument, identifying implications and recognising inconsistencies

Key words	What the key words mean
follow an argument	You can follow the train of thought of the writer.
identifying implications	You can identify what is hinted at but not said directly.
recognising inconsistencies	You are able to see when one argument, or part of an argument, clashes with another.

Follow an argument

Whether you are following someone else's argument or constructing your own, the way you need to think is similar. (Constructing an argument is covered in detail in the section of the book that deals with **writing to argue and persuade** on pages 108–109.)

Following an argument requires the same skills whatever reading task you are doing, whether it is for coursework, Paper 1, Paper 2 or literature. You need to consider:

✱ What is the main point that the writer is making?

✱ What are the minor points and how do they connect with the main point?

You need to look at the details and see how they connect with each other.

 **Where is this assessed?**

Following an argument is only assessed under examination conditions on Paper 1, but you also need to follow an argument when you read any text-based part of your English course.

Rubbish in leads to rubbish out

Government experts are blaming some of school children's bad behaviour on unhealthy school meals.

Most school dinners contain a lot of the foods linked to poor behaviour, but they also lack minerals that help to keep children emotionally balanced. One research group found that a primary school child eating five school dinners a week consumed 40% more salt, 28% more saturated fat and 20% more sugar than recommended levels.

Chocolate + sugar = trouble

Dr Neil Ward from Surrey University said that too much sugar and chocolate and not enough zinc and iron were linked to bad behaviour. Many experts believe that better diets could lead to fewer children being diagnosed with ADHD and needing drugs like Ritalin.

A Mars a day helps you...?

International studies showed that changing the diets of young offenders could reduce antisocial behaviour by 61% without side effects. In one institution, this was a simple matter of reducing the amount of sugar, chocolate, biscuits and fizzy drinks and giving mineral supplements. Dr Ward said, 'The governor said he could not believe we had taken a young man, who was inside for killing both his parents and who was constantly aggressive, and made him human.'

Task

What argument is being put forward in the passage on diet?

Examples of student performance

Student answer 1

Government experts blame bad behaviour on unhealthy school meals. School dinners contain 40% too much salt, 28% too much fat and 20% too much sugar. Dr Neil Ward also says that children eat too much chocolate.

Examiner's comment

This candidate has simply copied most of the original text and hardly changed the author's words. She has concentrated on the opening part of the article, so has not followed the whole argument. The examiner cannot tell if the candidate has understood the text. The answer would receive a Grade F.

Student answer 2

Government experts say that school dinners can lead to poor behaviour and that children are eating too much of the wrong sort of food. Dr Ward says that too much

sugar and chocolate are particularly bad and that better diets can lead to better behaviour. International studies have also shown how the behaviour of aggressive young men can be improved by changing diet.

Examiner's comment

This is a good example of a candidate who answers the question by looking at the whole argument. Although some of the writer's orginal words have been kept, there is clear use of the candidate's own words too. This candidate tries to sum up the whole argument by making a general point in the last sentence. He would be awarded a Grade C.

Student answer 3

The writer of this article set out to show how poor the diet of today's schoolchildren is and to show how changes can make a massive difference to performance and behaviour. He points to the poor nature of the food given to schoolchildren at lunchtime and argues that big improvements can be made by making quite simple changes. These changes to diet can also make big differences to young offenders.

Examiner's comment

This candidate has read the article, then asked what argument the writer wanted to get across to the reader. She has stood back from the article and has not simply paraphrased it. For example, instead of simply referring to school dinners, the candidate has referred to diet. She appreciates that the article is not really about schools or young offenders but about the effects of diet and nutrition on the young.

Note that the candidate has written about the same number of words as the previous student, but grasps the whole argument, not just the individual details. She would gain a Grade A.

Task

Sum up the argument of the following passage in one sentence only. Although you will not be asked to do this in the examination, it is a useful way of focusing your thoughts on the main thrust of the argument.

I like things that make sense. Having a monarchy reign over us in Britain has never made sense to me. I give you fair warning, you'll generally only get one side of the debate here. The main reason I don't directly address any good pro-monarchy arguments is because I believe that there aren't any! Reason and the needs of a modern country are on the side of republicans.

What about the success of the Golden Jubilee (or 'much ado about nothing' as I prefer to call it)? Please

don't confuse simultaneous joy at England's progress in the World Cup, or delight at music shows and fireworks (fire!) at Buckingham Palace, for deep-felt belief in the principle of hereditary rule.

The death of the Queen Mother allowed the Windsors to put on a show like only they can do and the guarding of the coffin gave the grandchildren an excuse to stand around, do nothing, and get paid for it. Any personal sympathy I had for the Windsors was slightly tainted when the execution of the Queen Mother's will highlighted the real tax status of the royals. Much has been made of the Queen paying taxes like everybody else, but, it seems, that equality doesn't stretch to the normal application of inheritance tax rules.

The republican cause is gathering momentum, getting stronger, and seems increasingly more acceptable to those in positions of power. Change is in the air. Be part of it by spreading the word.

Increasing democracy is by far the most important and powerful reason to ditch the monarchy. All other reasons either follow on from it or pale in comparison to the strength of the argument. Unfortunately, Britain has lagged behind other developed countries in both these areas. Our head of state (the Queen) and, until recently, the majority of the House of Lords assumed power and influence solely because of which families they were born in to. This makes Britain a relatively undemocratic country in an increasingly democratic world.

Identify implications and recognise inconsistencies

Identify implications means 'what is the writer hinting at?' Recognising inconsistencies means being able to see when one argument, or part of an argument, clashes with another.

Many jokes rely on implication — you are supposed to fill in the gaps yourself. For example:

> **Task**
>
> What is implied in the following statement?
>
> *'Did you mean to put on that top, or did you get dressed in the dark?'*

Reporter: Gordon, can we have a quick word please?
Gordon: Velocity.

> **Remember:**
> you imply *to*;
> you infer *from*.

 **Where is this assessed?**

Identifying implications and recognising inconsistencies is assessed mainly in English Paper 1 Section A, but this reading skill is vital when comparing poems in Paper 2 (poetry from different cultures) and poetry in the English Literature section.

How is this assessed?

This is usually assessed if you are required to read two or more items on the same subject. It is possible to identify implications and recognise inconsistencies within the same text, but it is more usual to be asked to look at two different texts.

Grade A	a complete answer which compares all parts of the question equally well
Grade C	a clear and structured attempt to compare
Grade F	an unstructured attempt to compare, but tends to identify features

Note how parts of these three basic grade descriptors are beginning to sound familiar.

How can you improve your answers?

To gain a grade higher than a D you have to make a clear comparison, finding either a similarity, a difference, or both. To make your comparisons clear you should learn how to use words and phrases such as those in the table below. You can also use comparatives such as bigger, louder, brighter, more colourful and clearer.

Showing similarities			
like	also	the same as	as
comparable to	corresponding to	too	resembles
both	similarly	likewise	in the same way
Showing differences			
but	however	in comparison with	conversely
on the other hand	contrasting with	unlike	whereas
nevertheless	although	except	yet

Task

Read the front page of *The Times* from 4 January 2005 (the same day as the *Daily Express* front page reproduced on page 18).

1 Identify the typical newspaper features on *The Times* front page, using appropriate technical terms.

Task (continued)

2 Compare the ways in which these two newspaper front pages are presented by copying out the following table and adding more information.

	Daily Express	*The Times*
Similarities	They both advertise what you will be able to read inside. They are the same size (tabloid).	
Differences	Not much text to read. Has a large kicker.	Has more detail. Has a smaller kicker.

3 Compare what the two papers actually write about, using a similar table to the one above.

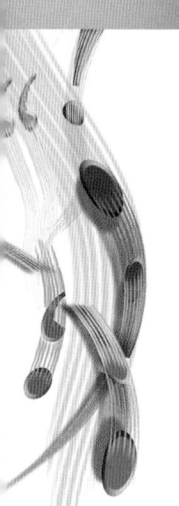

Picture caption reads:

Val Ledingham, a British woman, is comforted after finding the body of her son, Justin, at a mortuary in Krabi, Thailand

The cover copy reads:

The number of Britons feared killed by the Asian tsunami finally emerged last night as the Government disclosed that 199 people, including about 25 children, were probably dead.

Most British victims of the enormous wave that crashed into beach resorts nine days ago died in Thailand.

But any lingering hopes of the bodies of those still missing there being recovered were dashed last night when the authorities announced that they were calling off the search for those unaccounted for.

Of the 199, 40 are confirmed as dead. Of the remaining 159, 100 are missing in Thailand, 20 in Sri Lanka and 10 in the Maldives. The rest are unspecified. Britain will hold a three-minute silence for them tomorrow at a time not yet decided.

Jack Straw, the Foreign Secretary, said that 43 police had gone to Thailand to help in the search. Rescue leaders in the resort of Phuket have declared that there is no chance of finding anyone still alive, and that they do not have resources to continue the search for bodies.

The rescue operation is being scaled down and bulldozers sent in to clear damaged buildings in the worst-hit resorts, even though victims could be trapped inside.

Britons who have arrived in Thailand in the past 48 hours to search for the missing described this decision as 'heartless and far too hasty'.

Mr Straw said yesterday that because 'many of the bodies of the dead may sadly never be found, firm estimates of casualty figures remain difficult'.

However, the Foreign and Commonwealth Office has revised upwards its figure of 40 British deaths because there is now only a small possibility that anyone still missing will not have perished.

Tony Blair will attend his first meeting of the Government's South-East Asia emergency committee this morning after flying back from holiday in Egypt. In the Prime Minister's absence, Mr Straw defended the Government against accusations that it had donated less to the relief effort than the British public, saying that it would match the £70 million of donations. The Disasters Emergency Committee appeal will put a new figure on British donations today.

Gordon Brown will give a speech on Thursday setting out long-term aid to the region. An aide denied that money would be switched from other regions. The United Nations said last night that the death toll of about 150,000 could rise again as relief workers reached remote areas of western Sumatra.

Jan Egeland, the UN emergency relief coordinator, praised the outpouring of aid, which he put at more than $2 billion. 'We saw 2004 ending with nature at its very worst. We saw 2005 starting with humanity at its very best', he said.

When you come to write comparisons in the examination you could use the **Point, Example, Explain** structure (see pages 29–31), so your answer to question 3 might read: '**Both** newspapers lead with the tsunami story and the number of British deaths because it is obviously the most important story of the day. **However**, they differ about the number of deaths because nobody was quite sure as to the exact number. The *Express* rounds up to a more sensational '200', **whereas** *The Times* quotes a slightly more conservative, but precise, '199'. This might reflect something about the nature of these two newspapers.'

Examples of student performance

This is a typical exam question:

Compare the following items in the two newspapers:
* **presentation**
* **layout**
* **language**
* **purpose**

Task

Remind yourself of the three grade boundaries that have appeared throughout this section. Put these three students' responses to the above question into rank order and write the examiner's comment to go with each.

Student answer 1

The presentation of these two front pages is surprisingly similar. They both have large headlines, a similar picture and news of other features within the newspaper, but the *Daily Express* has very little copy to read on the front page.

The pages are laid out in the same way with very little difference between them, including the placing of the photographs in similar places. On the other hand, the *Daily Express* tends to look more like a magazine than a national daily newspaper.

There is very little language on the front page of the *Express*, but there is more in *The Times*.

The main purpose of the front page of the *Express* is to make people interested in buying the newspaper, which is similar to *The Times*, but *The Times* does include quite a lot of news as well.

Student answer 2

The surprising thing about these two front pages is how similar they are. Considering that *The Times* used to be a solely broadsheet newspaper, it has begun to take on

a lot of the characteristics of a tabloid. From a distance, the two newspapers look distressingly alike with their mastheads, headlines, photographs and use of colour. However, on closer study, *The Times* uses a lot less colour on its front page and does include a lot more copy. Additionally, *The Times* is presented like a smaller version of its broadsheet version: the *Express* is presented more like a popular magazine with its second-rate digital photograph.

As mentioned in the previous paragraph, the two newspapers are broadly similar in presentation and layout, but there are subtle differences. The *Daily Express* has a huge headline which looms across the front page and dwarfs the rest of the layout. It is understandable why this has been done, but it does take the paper into the realms of the *Sun* and the *Mirror*. The layout of *The Times* is similarly dominated by one feature; the photograph in this case. There is, however, a better balance in the layout between headline, copy and picture.

The language in the two articles is quite different. The *Express* tends to use sensational adjectives and nouns in its copy, like 'worst', 'biggest', 'appalling', 'back-lash' and 'catastrophe'. This use of language attempts to influence the reader's response and to sensationalise an already tragic situation. *The Times*, on the other hand, is more measured in its language and backs up its views with facts and quotations. There is an element of journalese in the headline, but it is more the sort of language expected of a quality daily newspaper that was once a broadsheet.

Finally, the two newspapers have similar purposes in that they both want to attract floating buyers to pick up their newspaper from the newsstand, but *The Times* is less blatant in its approach. The *Express* also has another purpose in its coverage of the tsunami story: it wants to criticise the Labour Party, and Tony Blair in particular, for its reaction to the tragedy. The final sentence of the copy, beginning 'News of the…', is a blatant attack and has little to do with the actual headline.

Student answer 3

The *Daily Express* has a photograph, a big headline and a personal horoscope free offer on the front. There is not very much writing, but there is quite a lot of colour. *The Times* has got more writing on the front and it has a big photograph of a mother being comforted after finding the body of her son. The writing in the *Express* is easy to understand, but there are quite a lot of long words. *The Times* is quite hard to understand as there is a lot of language.

The *Express* is laid out like a front page and *The Times* is more like a newspaper. I think the *Express* is laid out better.

The purpose of the *Express* is to tell people how many British people were killed in the tsunami wave tragedy. The purpose of *The Times* is to tell you a lot about a lot of different stories.

AO2(iv)

Select material appropriate to your purpose, collate material from different sources, and make cross-references

 **How is this assessed?**

Key words	What the key words mean
select material appropriate to your purpose	You can choose quotations or make references that suit the purpose of your writing.
collate material from different sources	You can bring together references from more than one text.
make cross-references	You can refer to an idea in one text and then link it to a similar or contrasting idea from another text.

Select material appropriate to your purpose

When you are writing about texts, you need to make clear precisely what it is you are referring to. Use quotations and/or references to illustrate the points you make. You must do this whether you are writing about English Literature, writing an English coursework assignment on Shakespeare or responding to the reading questions on English Paper 1 Section A and English Paper 2 Section A. In each case you need to:

* make a **Point (P)**
* find an **Example (E)**
* **Explain (E)**

> **Note:** It is useful to keep a quotation book.

For more detailed advice on how to use quotations in English Literature answers, see Chapter 2.

 **Where is this assessed?**

AO2(iv) is assessed whenever you read, so it is vitally important.

 **How can you improve your answers?**

The skill lies in finding the particular words that illustrate your point. If you quote too much, it gives the impression that you do not know which words you need. Supposing, for example, you quoted an entire poem. The words you need would obviously be in the poem somewhere, but copying the whole poem out would indicate to the examiner that you don't know where the best quotation is and so you have copied it all to be on the safe side.

You should make references or choose quotations that are **short and precise**. Read the following passage, the opening of 'Superman and Paula Brown's New Snowsuit', a short story by Sylvia Plath in the AQA *Anthology* (pages 63–67).

The year the war began I was in the fifth grade at the Annie F. Warren Grammar School in Winthrop, and that was the winter I won the prize for drawing the best Civil Defence signs. That was also the winter of Paula Brown's new snowsuit, and even now, thirteen years later, I can recall the changing colours of those days, clear and definite as patterns seen through a kaleidoscope.

I lived on the bay side of town, on Johnson Avenue, opposite the Logan Airport, and before I went to bed each night, I used to kneel by the west window of my room and look over to the lights of Boston that blazed and blinked far off across the darkening water. The sunset flaunted its pink flag above the airport, and the sound of waves was lost in the perpetual droning of the planes. I marvelled at the moving beacons on the runway and watched, until it grew completely dark, the flashing red and green lights that rose and set in the sky like shooting stars. The airport was my Mecca, my Jerusalem. All night I dreamed of flying.

> ## Task
>
> Find the most appropriate **brief** quotation to support the following point:
>
> *'The writer remembers how she was fascinated by the changing colours she saw as a young girl.'*

Using quotations: three levels

Read the poem 'Nothing's Changed' by Tatamkhulu Afrika (page 6 of the AQA *Anthology*). Explain how the writer's choice of language helps to get his message across that nothing has changed.

An answer to this question should fulfil three criteria:
* identify a feature of the writer's language
* illustrate this feature with an appropriate quotation
* explain how the feature relates to the writer's purpose

Below are three examples of student answers to the question. They show increasing skill in the use of quotations. Notice how the best of these answers actually quotes fewer words than the weakest answer but does much more with the quotations.

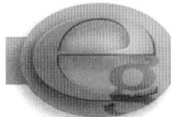

Examples of student performance

Level 1 (Grade F)

The poet uses a lot of language to help to get his message across. For example:

> Small round hard stones click
> under my heels,
> seeding grasses thrust
> bearded seeds
> into trouser cuffs, cans,
> trodden on, crunch

Examiner's comment

This answer only **identifies** a quotation. It does no more than turn the question around and then copy out the first stanza. The quotation is pointless as it is nothing more than copying.

Level 2 (Grade C)

The poet uses similes and metaphors to help get his message across. 'Brash with glass,/name flaring like a flag' is a quotation that shows how the poet uses language figuratively to help conjure up a picture in the reader's mind. The image of the name of the restaurant looking like a flag makes the reader think of American imperialism and the way they always fly the stars and stripes.

Examiner's comment

This answer **identifies** a quotation and **illustrates** it. However, the quotation has been chosen as an example of literary devices — similes and metaphors — but the poet's message is not actually discussed. The image of the flag is identified, the link with American imperialism is made, but the point of this connection is not explained.

Level 3 (Grade A)

Monosyllabic words are used from the first line — 'Small round hard stones click' — and are used throughout the poem. This creates the feeling of a pulse and suggests a sense of throbbing anger that leads up to the moment when 'Hands burn' for a weapon.

Examiner's comment

This candidate **identifies** a quotation, **illustrates** and **explains** it. The answer shows that the whole poem has been read and understood. The two quotations are used in such a way that they become part of the comment.

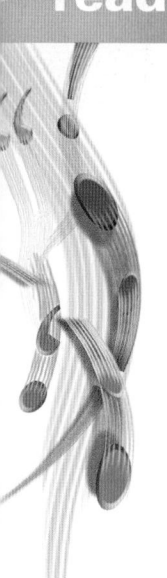

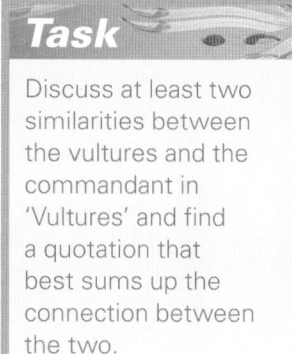

> ### Task
>
> Read the poem 'Vultures' on page 10 of the AQA *Anthology*.
>
> Find precise quotations (of no more than three words each) to illustrate the following aspects of the poem:
> * the atmosphere and mood
> * a feeling of disgust
> * a sense of affection
> * an image of evil

Collate material from different sources

A sign of a good candidate is the ability to collate (bring together) relevant pieces of information from different places. This could mean:

* selecting material from different places within one poem
* bringing together similar ideas from a leaflet and an article on Paper 1
* finding similar or contrasting ideas in two different poems on Paper 2
* choosing quotations from post-1914 and pre-1914 poems for English Literature

In fact, whenever you are writing about a text you should be alert to collating material from different places.

> **Do not** become restricted to discussing only one small area of a text.

Make cross-references

This skill appears in all of the mark schemes for English and English Literature from Grade C upwards. In other words, if you do not make cross-references you will not get as far as Grade C.

When cross-referencing you are comparing and contrasting, and finding similarities and differences, to show links between different texts or different parts of the same text. (See the detailed advice on how to do this on pages 25–27.)

Once you have learned to use cross-references within one text you can apply the same skill and process to comparing more than one text. Examination questions on poetry and prose texts vary but the approach that you take to cross-referencing will be the same.

> ### Task
>
> Discuss at least two similarities between the vultures and the commandant in 'Vultures' and find a quotation that best sums up the connection between the two.

Task

Read 'Unrelated Incidents' and 'Half-Caste', on pages 12 and 13 of the AQA *Anthology*. What are the similarities and differences between these two poems?

Use the chart to help you answer the question.

	'Unrelated Incidents'	'Half-Caste'
Meanings		
Structure/ layout		
Use of language		
Different cultures		

This sort of chart will also help you prepare for the examination.

Cross-referencing: three levels

As for the use of quotations, there are generally three levels of skill in making cross-references. The following three student answers to the task above demonstrate increasing levels of skill. The first two attempts show the simplest ways of making cross-references. To respond at the highest level, you need to show that you are aware of many ways in which two texts can be compared.

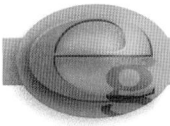

Examples of student performance

Level 1 (Grade F)

'Unrelated Incidents' is about a Scottish man who is annoyed that Scottish people are never asked to read the news by the BBC and he is annoyed that people do not take Scottish people seriously because of the way they speak.

'Half-Caste' is about a half-caste standing on one leg and shouting at people that they shouldn't judge people by the colour of their skin.

Examiner's comment

This answer shows a simple **identification of ideas**. The two comments are completely separate. There is no obvious link between them.

Level 2 (Grade C/D)

'Unrelated Incidents' is about how you should not judge somebody by the way they speak. The poet, Tom Leonard, is especially annoyed that a Scottish voice is never heard reading the BBC News. This is about a sort of prejudice. John Agard is also writing about a sort of prejudice but in this case he is talking about the way people are treated because of the colour of their skin.

Examiner's comment

The answer shows **identification of ideas and linking of comments**. The candidate tries to compare the two writers' ideas. These comparisons can be seen clearly through the use of 'but' and 'also'. Appropriate statements are linked.

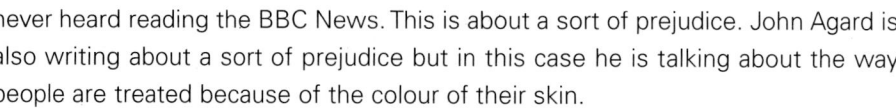

Task

Read the following answer to the question on the Leonard and Agard poems and identify all the places where the links between the two poems are made clear.

Level 3 (Grade A)

These two poems are nominally on the same subject (prejudice), but they have very different purposes. The first poem by Leonard is about the way people are prejudged by the way they speak, as in lines 15–21, but there is a deeper undercurrent of meaning that links the meaning, shape, language and cultural outrage: and that is the poem's strength. It appears to be quite a simple rant about the way that the Scots are treated by people with BBC accents, but it has a wider significance about the narrow way in which we view anyone with a difference. This wider significance is also obvious in Agard's poem, which is not just about him being annoyed about being judged as a half-caste; in my opinion, it is about how people have very narrow views about anyone with a different way of looking at things, like Picasso or Tchaikovsky. Agard is inviting the reader to listen to 'de other half/of my story'.

Again, the two poems are ostensibly laid out quite differently on the page, but the two poets use the different ways that they have chosen to lay their poems out in order to make an important point about the meanings of their poems. Leonard is challenging the accepted way of writing a poem by choosing this very narrow, limited shape. He is breaking away from the traditional form of the poem in order to make his angry point. It is almost as if the shape of the poem is saying that you don't have to read from the narrow script, or autocue, but that you can actually have your own view about things and that it is alright.

Similarly, Agard uses a non-traditional structure in order to make his non-traditional point about racial prejudice. His repetition of the phrase 'explain yuself' makes the reader justify reasons they may have for judging something simply from outward appearances. This poem is only half of the story and this incompleteness is mirrored by its shape on the page.

The first poet uses language that fits in with its perceived purpose, which is to show that you can make a perfectly valid point if you speak in a non-BBC accent. The poet is saying that truth is a matter of cultural identity and that the way you speak is linked to your self-image. That is why the poet ends with the words 'belt up': he is so annoyed that anyone would have such a narrow cultural stereotype. Agard is the same in that he uses his own cultural patois to make the point that he is proud of the way that he speaks and confronts the prejudiced reader with the strength and colour of his own way of speaking. He, too, is exasperated and uses the phrase 'ah rass' to show his continuous sense of anger, which cannot even be stopped by punctuation. The poet uses enjambement so that the lines all run into each other with token forward slashes to help the reader to make sense of the poem's shape. It is interesting to note that Leonard also abuses the normal rules of punctuation by not using any capital letters at all, except for BBC. He, too, is exasperated and refuses to use conventional punctuation in order to make a point.

Both poets are making a very similar point about prejudice, and although they are writing from completely different cultural backgrounds, they both link meaning with form and language to make their point. It does not matter that they are writing from different cultural backgrounds because they are both making the same point. Neither wants to be judged as half a person for some outward reason that does not really matter. These poems are not about individual people, they are about all of us.

Where is this assessed?

The use of cross-references is assessed mainly under examination conditions in Paper 1, but this reading skill is vital when comparing poems in Paper 2 (poetry from different cultures) and in English Literature poetry.

How is this assessed?

This skill can only be assessed if you are required to read two or more items on the same subject. It is possible to 'collate materials from different sources and make cross-references' within the same text, but it is more usual to be asked to look at two or more texts.

Grade A	a complete answer which compares all parts of the question equally well
Grade C	a clear and structured attempt to compare
Grade F	an unstructured attempt to compare, but tends to identify features

AO2(v)

Understand and evaluate how writers use linguistic, structural and presentational devices to achieve their effects, and comment on ways language varies and changes

Key words	What the key words mean
understand and evaluate how writers use linguistic, structural and presentational devices to achieve their effects	You can comment on the ways that writers use forms of language to create effects. You can appreciate how the structure of a piece of writing can have an effect on the way you read it. You can comment on the way that the presentation on the page influences the reader.
comment on ways language varies and changes	You can recognise that language changes over time and that writers can choose to exploit changes in language to create effects.

Although the second part of this AO is only really looked at in English Literature, there are occasions when it might be assessed in Paper 1, so it is discussed on pages 40–44.

Understand and evaluate how writers use linguistic, structural and presentational devices to achieve their effects

Pegs for life

The best way to keep those first teeth looking white

Contains a patented child-friendly flouroxide formula to keep those first teeth white and healthy. Don't let your child's smile let you down. Use *Pegs* to keep that smile on his face!

Pegs

Task A

Here is a list of the ten most common presentational devices that are used in the kinds of documents you will see on Paper 1.

Identify as many as you can in the following advertisement for Pegs toothpaste:

* headlines   * italics
* sub-headings   * fonts
* illustrations   * columns
* colour   * bullets
* bold   * word art

This skill is assessed under examination conditions on Paper 1, in pre-1914 literature, drama, prose and poetry tasks, and may be used in the media writing task.

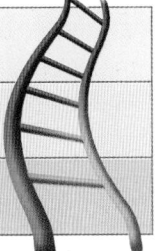

Grade A provides a clear, evaluative **judgement** about the use of two or three devices
Grade C clearly attempts to **identify**, **explain** or **evaluate** the devices
Grade F attempts to **identify** the presentational device and tends to list

To improve your performance you should:

❋ answer the question you have been given

❋ read the material and choose two or three devices to focus on

❋ develop and sustain a response — or, in other words, say a lot about a little

This is exactly the same way in which to score high marks as when you are asked to write about linguistic or presentational devices in poetry in Paper 2 and in the Literature paper.

Task B

Read the Pegs advertisement again, but this time choose three presentational devices to focus on and explain why you think each is effective or not.

Task C

1 Identify one organisational device in the Pegs advertisement and write it down.

Organisational devices include:

❋ paragraphs ❋ bullet points
❋ layout ❋ columns
❋ sub-headings ❋ call outs etc. (a call out is like a speech bubble)

2 Explain how the writer uses this organisational device and say whether you think it works or not.

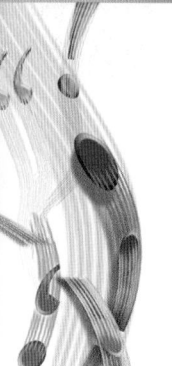

Task D

1 Identify one linguistic device in the Pegs advertisement and write it down.

Linguistic devices include:
* use of technical/scientific terms
* formal/informal style
* tense (present, past, future)
* tone (serious, ironic, persuasive, humorous etc.)
* restricted semantic field (a technical, linguistic term for the writer choosing to use words of a particular type, e.g. all to do with violence, war, nature)

2 Explain how the writer uses this linguistic device and say whether you think it works or not.

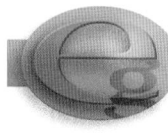

Examples of student performance

Task A

The advert uses a colourful picture of a young child, a colourful, friendly font, bold writing and a headline.

Examiner's comment

Task A is a Foundation Tier question which is only testing lower-level reading skills. The answer, therefore, will simply **identify** and write down the presentational devices. This student would achieve an F/G grade because of the nature of the question.

Task B

There are several presentational devices used in this advertisement, so I will choose the three most noticeable ones and explain how I think they work. In my opinion, the picture of the child's face with the toothy smile is the most obvious presentational device. The picture reinforces the main message from the manufacturers of the toothpaste, which is that it makes your child's teeth white. The reader's eyes are drawn by the child's smile and we are almost forced to read the copy and skim the rest of the devices used by the advertisers.

Second, the font is sans serif, which advertisers often use to make their copy less formal and more inviting to the reader.

Finally, bright blues are used in the advertisement portraying a sense of hygiene and cleanliness, as well as brightness and freshness. So, overall, I believe that the presentational devices add to the meaning of the advertisement, which is what they should do.

1

Examiner's comment

This is a high-level answer because it 'says a lot about a little'. The student fulfils all of the criteria for an A/A* answer and addresses the question in some detail. The candidate uses technical vocabulary (like 'copy' and 'font'), which allows explanation of the advertiser's devices. Just knowing the terminology would earn the candidate few marks: using the terms to explain how the advertisers use the devices helps the student in her conceptualisation, or higher-level idea formation. Note how the student uses the structuring words 'second' and 'finally' to help the examiner through the answer.

Task C

The main organisational device used by the writers of this advertisement is the para-graph, or block, of writing. It is written in dark blue against a light blue background so that it stands out. It is placed next to the photograph of the cute child so that your eyes are naturally drawn to it. The paragraph is not long and includes some high-lighted writing so we do not miss the main message. The whole advert is organised like a newspaper, with a headline, a picture and some copy.

Examiner's comment

This is not as good as the answer to Task B, but it would gain a mark in the C/B band. The candidate clearly attempts to answer the question and explains the use of the main organisational device on the page. To gain more marks, the candidate could have gone into more detail, or explained more about the overall layout of the page. This was a good point that was undeveloped.

Task D

The language in this advertisement is overtly persuasive and sounds like the tran-script of a television advertisement, with its short sentences, highlighted words and catchphrases. The main linguistic device used by the advertisers, apart from the scientific-sounding additive, is the way they try to make parents feel guilty. 'Don't let your child's smile let you down' sends a subtle, almost coded, message to parents that they could be guilty of neglecting their children's teeth if they don't use this product. Naming the product 'Pegs' is another subtle way of engaging parents' inter-est, as this is a commonly used term for children's teeth.

Examiner's comment

This is a reasonably detailed response to the question, but does not go into enough detail on any of the valid points made. However, the student clearly shows that he is able to shape and absorb the material to answer the question. In addition, there is evidence of some technical linguistic vocabulary (transcript, catchphrases, coded), which the student uses successfully. This answer would gain a mark at the top end of the B/C band.

Comment on ways language varies and changes

Where is this assessed?

Once more, this part of AO2(v) is only assessed under examination conditions in Paper 1 on some occasions, but it is usually covered in pre-1914 prose text coursework, the pre-1914 drama text coursework and the pre-1914 poetry examination question.

How is this assessed?

Grade A	a complete answer with the material being shaped and absorbed for purpose with a convincing use of technical terminology
Grade C	a clear and structured response to the question which selects and comments on different aspects of how language has changed
Grade F	an unstructured attempt to engage with the task, with the student tending to paraphrase and to identify examples of language change

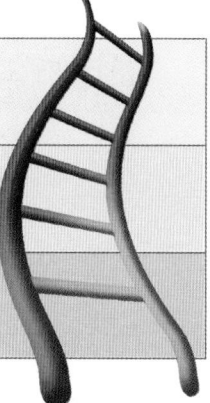

How can you improve your answers?

There are a number of different ways of getting better at this particular skill. Here are some suggestions:

* carry over skills from pre-1914 prose and pre-1914 poetry
* carry over skills from media studies
* use source material in your history course as comparative texts with modern non-fiction and media

---

Task E

Compare how the:
* layout
* language
* purpose
* audience
of the two advertisements for skin care (opposite) show that they were written at very different times. (8 marks)

(Note that on Paper 1, when you have to answer a question that has bullet points, spend an equal amount of time on each point. The number of minutes you should spend on a question is approximately twice the number of marks available. So for Task E, you should spend about 4 minutes on each of the bullets.)

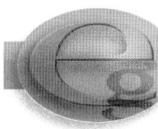

Examples of student performance

Student answer 1

The 'Nivea' advert shows a young woman's face which is perfect and has no pimples or spots. Probably, they have air-brushed out any skin problems so that she looks perfect. This is aimed at women and there is not much language at all. The 'Pomeroy Skin Food' advert has a lot more language and it does not even show a woman's face. It suggests that you will look like a lady in a boudoir if you use this skin product.

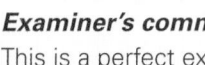

Examiner's comment

This is a perfect example of an 'unstructured response' that simply 'paraphrases', or tells the story of the adverts. The student does not compare, but just **juxtaposes** responses to the two items. This student would gain 2/3 marks for this level of response, which would translate to a Grade E/F.

Student answer 2

The layout of the two advertisements is very different. The Nivea advert is mainly taken up with a full-face picture of a young woman with perfect skin and with a pot

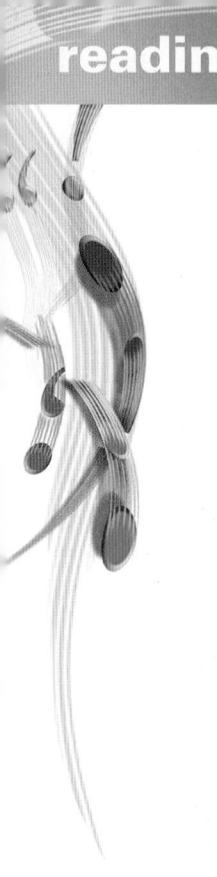

of the cream centrally placed and a headline at the top of the page. On the other hand, the Pomeroy advert is dominated by a drawing of a woman in a boudoir, with about the same amount of writing, but in a much smaller space. This makes the layout of this advert look cluttered.

Similarly, the language used in both adverts is very different. The language used in the Nivea advert is very definite as it tells the reader that it is 'THE BEST' and that 'WRINKLES HATE IT'. This style of telling the reader what to think is repeated throughout the advert. The Pomeroy advert uses more formal language which is because it was written in the past.

The purpose of both adverts is to sell their product and to make rather inflated claims for the product they are selling. They also both try to suggest that if you use their product then you will look like the person in the advert.

Again, the audiences of both adverts are similar in that they are both aimed at women who believe that they have a problem with wrinkles and other skin problems. However, the Pomeroy product is aimed at 'posher' women than the Nivea cream because the woman in the picture is in a boudoir and is dressed like a lady. Also, the language is posher in the Pomeroy advert because it uses words like 'eradicates' and it also uses alliteration in the headline.

Examiner's comment

This is a clear C-grade response because the student addresses each of the bullet points in a structured way and actually answers the question, which is to compare how the two adverts show that they were written at different times. The comparison words and phrases have been highlighted to make it obvious that the student is addressing the main objective of this question.

The student is, however, rather mechanical in responding to each bullet and almost identifies each difference or similarity without really commenting on it. This is a good example of how a student can gain marks by attempting the question as set and by applying a structure to the response. In this case, that structure is a paragraph about each of the bullets and a comparison within each paragraph.

Student answer 3

It is very obvious that these two adverts were written at different times even from a cursory glance, but it is interesting to examine the ways in which they are similar and different. The most obvious difference between the two is the size and the ways in which the images of women have been integrated into the layouts. The Nivea advert is 'in your face' in that it is dominated by an image of the woman's perfect skin. This layout technique allows the advertisers to make the page resemble a mirror in which the reader can compare her own image. This comparison is bound to be detrimental. The much smaller Pomeroy advert is also dominated by the female form, but this time, the reader is given a lifestyle image which suggests that if the reader

uses Pomeroy products, she will end up being like this lady in a boudoir. The layout definitely suggests a different period in history, because the layout coyly shows a lady's back and only suggests a hint of skin by showing her neck and forearms. This coyness points to a difference in attitude and social perspective.

It is, however, in the language that there are the greatest differences. The Nivea advert is peremptory in its style in that it *tells* the reader, by using a definite form of the verb (e.g. 'hate', 'reduces', 'Proven'). It also uses dubious scientific-sounding language to back up its claims that it gets rid of wrinkles. By using scientific-sounding terms, like 'Q10' and 'unique Energy Complex', it persuades the reader that the whole product has a scientific basis. By personifying the product ('WRINKLES HATE IT'), the advertiser conveys power onto the product by making it something that wrinkles actively hate. On the other hand, the Pomeroy product is driven more by narrative in its approach. The style is more personal as it addresses the reader directly; even though it is in the third person, it is quite personal. There is also an interesting use of alliteration in the heading which stresses the fact that the reader will share the lifestyle of the lady whose back is showing.

Both adverts have the same overall purpose, which is to sell their product to women and to help them with their skin-care problems. The direct gaze of the Nivea woman suggests an openness and directness, which is reflected by the almost magic qualities of the cream because it shines and glistens in the pot. With its scientific language and perfect appearance, it suggests a miracle cure from wrinkles. The Pomeroy cream also suggests a sort of miracle in that it tries to tie the reader in by suggesting that they will never be able to live without it after having used it ('it is impossible to imagine'). Its purpose is also linked with language, audience and layout, because the advertiser is attempting to connect all aspects of the advert's appeal.

Finally, the audiences are obviously similar because they are both unashamedly aimed at women and prey on a woman's fear of ageing and getting wrinkles. They are both aimed at the same age range, but they are subtly aimed at different social classes. The Nivea advert is more universal in its appeal to all classes. However, the Pomeroy product, even by dint of its name, is aiming at a more affluent audience. The layout and language all suggest an upper-middle-class audience, especially the address and name of the person to whom all correspondence should be sent.

Examiner's comment

This is a complete answer which comments on different aspects of each bullet and goes into some detail. 'Saying a lot about a little' is often a descriptor for performance in the A/A* grade boundary.

The other strength of this answer, which lifts it into this grade boundary, is the way it **links** the different elements listed in the bullet points. This is the ability 'to absorb and shape'. In practice, it means that the student can read a whole item;

absorb it; keep it in his/her mind's eye; compare different aspects of the first item with a second one; then shape the response to fit the actual demands of the question. This student shows how the apparently separate bullet points are all, in fact, linked, and is beginning to make 'big picture links' between meaning, layout, presentation etc. These links are equally important when reading non-fiction, media, poetry, prose or drama.

Task F

Now use the skills that you have learned above to answer the following question:

In what ways are the two poems 'October' by Gillian Clarke and 'Tichborne's Elegy' by Charles Tichborne, on pages 30 and 48 of the AQA *Anthology*, the same and different in the ways that they use language? Is it important that they were written at different times?

Responding to literature

Chapter 2

You will find yourself writing about literature in the following situations:

Assessment area	Exam/coursework	Texts
Poems from different cultures	Exam (Paper ....)	
Pre- and post-1914 poetry	Exam (Paper ....)	
Set prose text	Exam (Paper ....)	
Drama pre-1914	Coursework	
Drama post-1914	Coursework	
Prose pre-1914	Coursework	

Not every student will be reading exactly the same texts, so you need to make sure you know which ones you will be studying.

Task

Find out from your teacher where you are examined on the different assessment areas and which texts you will be using. Copy out the above table and complete:

❋ the exam paper and section for each exam element

❋ which texts you will be writing about (there will be several in some cases)

No matter which piece of literature you are writing about, you need broadly the same set of skills. Of course, writing about poetry makes different demands upon you from writing about a novel, but there are still many common things that you can say about any literary text. Any piece of writing about literature requires that you use the appropriate technical terms, and you will quickly see how these terms apply to writing about poetry, prose and drama.

In this chapter you will find:

❋ explanations of technical terms

❋ advice on using technical terms

❋ sample passages with worked examples

❋ tasks for you to attempt

The examples in this chapter are taken from poetry, prose and plays. Each of these literary forms has its own particular qualities, but they have many things in common too. For example, poets, novelists and playwrights all use imagery. Once you have learned to comment on imagery in one form of literature you can apply this skill to the other forms.

Making sense of the words

One of the things that often puts students off studying literature is the number of technical terms that are used, such as onomatopoeia, imagery and alliteration. These terms are useful when writing about a text, but they do not necessarily help you to read a text.

Compare this to football. Simply knowing what all of the playing positions are — fullback, midfield, centre forward and so on — will not help you learn to play football. Once you come to play in a match these positions become important, but they are not all the game is about. Writing about literature is similar. Knowing a list of technical terms can be useful; just trotting them out with no real understanding of the way they are used is pointless.

> Think about purpose and audience.

Writers are sometimes known as 'wordsmiths'. Words are what writers use; they manipulate them for a purpose. You need to consider words and what they can do.

What's in a name?

Your surname may well have had an obvious meaning in the past — butcher, fletcher, cartwright — but it is now simply a name.

So why do parents spend time thinking about the name of a new child? Is it because names can have a different sort of meaning to that you can find in a dictionary of names? 'Jacqueline' is from Hebrew and means 'supplanter'. To supplant is to dispossess and take the place of — but does this mean no girl called Jacqueline can be trusted?

> ### Task
>
> Write down what you think the differences are between the following two versions of the same name:
>
> ❋ Michael/Mike
>
> ❋ Constance/Connie
>
> ❋ Katherine/Kate
>
> ❋ Edward/Teddy
>
> ❋ James/Jimmy
>
> ❋ Susan/Sue

If you can see differences between the versions of names in the task box, then you are already thinking about **connotation**.

Why is it Billy Casper in *A Kestrel for a Knave* and not William Casper?

Connotation

Looking at the connotations of words — their additional meanings — is a useful way to begin exploring a text. You might not have used the term before but you will already be sensitive to the connotations of words in everyday life. For example, someone who refuses to change his/her mind could be described as:

Positive connotation	Negative connotation
determined	stubborn
resolute	obstinate
strong-minded	pig-headed

The person's behaviour would be the same in each of the cases, but how this is put across can change the way you think about their actions.

Even letters or numbers can have connotations. Consider the letter 'X'. Many technical devices have the letter 'X' in their name to make them sound scientific. Why is it an X-box and not a D-box? What other connotations does 'X' have?

Task

Look at the Gladys soap advert. It is on an advertising billboard in India.

1 What do you think the target audience is and why?

2 What connotations does the name Gladys have in the UK today?

3 What connotations do you think the name Gladys might have in India?

4 How can the same name suggest different things?

Understanding that writers use words with different connotations is an important step in getting a feel for the way words affect the reader. For example, one of the most famous poems written in English is William Blake's 'The Tyger' (1794). It has been interpreted in many different ways.

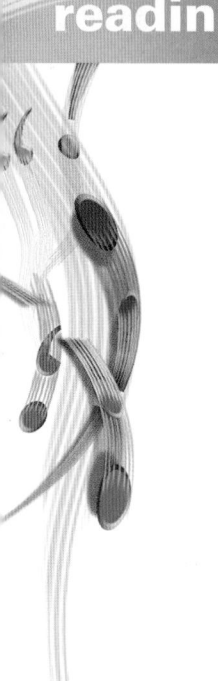

The Tyger

Tyger! Tyger! burning bright
In the forests of the night,
What immortal hand or eye
Could frame thy fearful symmetry?

In what distant deeps or skies
Burnt the fire of thine eyes?
On what wings dare he aspire?
What the hand, dare seize the fire?

And what shoulder, and what art,
Could twist the sinews of thy heart?
And when thy heart began to beat,
What dread hand? And what dread feet?

What the hammer? What the chain?
In what furnace was thy brain?
What the anvil? What dread grasp
Dare its deadly terrors clasp?

When the stars threw down their spears,
And water'd heaven with their tears,
Did he smile his work to see?
Did he who made the Lamb make thee?

Tyger! Tyger! burning bright
In the forests of the night,
What immortal hand or eye
Dare frame thy fearful symmetry?

The poem has always had an almost hypnotic effect on readers, but at the same time is notoriously difficult to explain. We can, however, discover much about its meaning simply by considering the connotations of its vocabulary:

* **tyger** refers to a particular species of animal, but also suggests things that are ferocious, mysterious and exotic
* **burning** could have many meanings, for example passion, glowing in the dark, destroying
* when used with 'burning', **bright** suggests intensity, effects of light, something shining gloriously; bright has religious associations too, i.e. the light of Christ
* **forests** are wild, mysterious places, dark and impenetrable
* **night** can be associated with evil, mystery and fear

You can probably think of more associations of your own, and as you do so you will become aware of how Blake builds up a pattern of sense and feeling. If you think about all the possible connotations of the words in the first two lines alone, you will start to see a strange and even disturbing set of ideas.

Task

Let your imagination loose on the following words and write down the thoughts and emotions they suggest to you:

* distant   * chain
* burnt   * furnace
* twist   * hammer
* anvil   * lamb

Positive and negative connotation

You might have noticed that some of the words in 'The Tyger' have positive connotations (e.g. 'bright') whereas others have decidedly negative connotations (e.g. 'tears'). Sorting words according to whether they have positive or negative connotations can be helpful when you are making sense of what a writer is trying to do. A piece of writing that contains many positive words might suggest hope, optimism, joy etc. A piece of writing that is full of negative words could suggest gloom, depression, hopelessness etc.

Task

Read the two poems below. Both of them deal with the natural landscape.

Think about the connotations of the words the poets use and write a few sentences on each poem, commenting on the feelings that each poet is trying to convey.

'Twas one of those dark, cloudy days
That sometimes come in summer's blaze,
When heaven drops not, when earth is still,
And deeper green is on the hill.

Lonely at her window sitting,
While the evening stole away;
Fitful winds, foreboding, flitting
Through a sky of cloudy grey.

There are two trees in a lonely field;
They breathe a spell to me;
A dreary thought their dark boughs yield,
All waving solemnly.

Untitled, Emily Brontë, 1838

Now the meadow water smokes,
And the hedgerow's dripping oaks
Pitter-patter all around
And dimple the once dusty ground;
The spinners' threads about the weeds
Are hung with little drops in beads;
Clover silver-green becomes,
And purple-blue surrounds the plums,
And every place breathes fresh and fair
When morning pays her visit there.
The waterfowl with suthering wing
Dive down the river, splash and spring
Up to the very clouds again
That sprinkle scuds of coming rain,
That fly and drizzle all the day
Till dripping grass is turned to grey;
The various clouds now move or lie
Like mighty travellers in the sky,
All mountainous and ridged and curled,
That may have travelled round the world.

'Morning Showers', John Clare, 1825

Not only poets use connotation. In the prose passage below the author describes an airfield in the opening of a novel.

> Snow covered the airfield.
> It had come in from the north, in the mist, driven by the night wind, smelling of the sea. There it would stay all winter, threadbare on the grey earth, an icy, sharp dust; not thawing and freezing, but static like a year without seasons. The changing mist, like the smoke of war, would hang over it, swallow up now a hangar, now the radar hut, now the machines; release them piece by piece, drained of colour, black carrion on a white desert.
>
> John Le Carré, *The Looking Glass War*, 1965

Take the word 'carrion' from the extract. Carrion is dead and rotting flesh. This word alone carries unpleasant connotations that can influence the way you see the whole passage.

Task

Look at the connotations in the passage above and say what mood the writer is trying to create.

This is the opening of a spy novel. Can you guess why the author describes the airfield in this way?

2

Technical terms

You have seen that we respond constantly to connotation in everyday life and that writers use this to create effects upon the reader. In the same way, authors use other techniques or devices to create effects. As you begin to write about literature it is helpful to equip yourself with the special language that is used to comment on it. This section will help you to become familiar with the technical terms that are used when discussing literature. Work through the terms until you understand them and can apply them confidently to the poems, plays and prose texts you are studying.

> **Do** use technical terms, but make sure you understand them.

Imagery

One of the most notable qualities of the language in novels, plays and especially poetry is the amount of imagery that is used. This is usually far more than appears in everyday speech or in essays.

An image is a likeness of something. For example, a photograph is an image of the object that was photographed. When you look at a picture of a statue, you know you are not looking at the statue itself. In some cases you will be able to trust that the photograph is a true likeness of the subject. If the photograph of the statue appears in a respectable daily newspaper as part of its coverage of a new museum display, then it is probably safe to say that if you visit the museum the statue will look exactly like it does in the photograph.

The statue itself might not be a realistic represen-tation of its subject. You need to think about whether an image is *realistic* or *idealised*. Artists have many reasons for portraying someone or something in unrealistic ways. You need to con-sider what statement the artist or writer was trying to make and how far this has been successful.

Look at the three statues shown here. Statue A is Donatello's *David*; statue B is the *Venus de Milo*, thought to be by Alexandros of Antioch; and statue C is *Alison Lapper Pregnant* by Marc Quinn. Do you think statue A is an entirely realistic image of its subject? It is likely that the sculptor was trying to portray an ideal human being. Are statues B and C also idealised images of women?

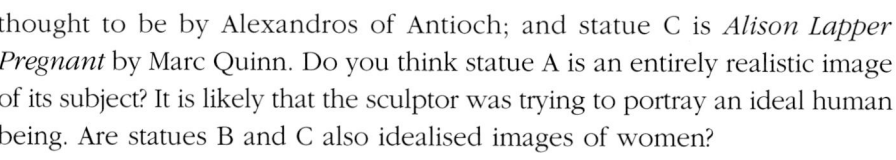

Task

1 Look at statues A, B and C. Think about the statements the sculptors might have been trying to make. Write down three points about the way each statue represents a person or a group of people. (Remember that you are really thinking about images and how they can be interpreted in different ways.)

2 Write an essay about the following statement: 'Artists cannot be trusted to portray the real world.'

Poets create images using words. When you are writing about poetry, think about the reason the poem was written and see if you can find a link between the poet's intentions and the kinds of images in the poem. If the poem is full of images of death and despair, for example, it would not be aimed at an audience of little children and might reflect the poet's own despondency.

Look at the film stills and match the image with the correct film genre:

❋ romantic comedy
❋ horror
❋ war film
❋ adventure

You probably found this easy, because you are familiar with the types of images that filmmakers use. Writers do the same, but their images are formed using words. There are two main types of image that writers use: **simile** and **metaphor**.

Simile

A simile is a word picture that makes a direct comparison between two things, for example 'a soft round beast as brown as clay' and 'two small paws like hands flew out'. Similes use '**like**' or '**as**' to make the comparison.

You need to consider what the simile is being used to do. Note that:

✳ The first part of the simile identifies the subject and is usually easy to understand.
✳ The second part helps the reader to picture the image more clearly and to make greater sense of the ideas behind it.

> ### Task
> Complete each of the following similes:
> 1 He was as pale as…
> 2 She spoke quietly like…
> 3 Time passes like…
> 4 Creeping along…
> 5 Its skin was…

Metaphor

Images that do not use 'like' or 'as' are called metaphors. A metaphor is a way of describing one thing in terms of something else. For example, you could write 'The ball moved through the air like a sailing ship moves through the water', but it is more elegant to say 'The ball sailed through the air'. Of course a ball cannot literally sail, but we can easily form a picture of the motion of the ball by comparing it to that of a sailing ship. Metaphors allow us to **compress** meaning. They can suggest meanings that cannot easily be conveyed by any other means.

You need to consider what the metaphor is being used to do. You will not pick up many marks simply for spotting a metaphor.

> ### Task
> Read the short poem below. It is almost entirely metaphors. Identify each metaphor and write down what you think each one suggests.

> ### Task
> Write a suitable metaphor for each of the following:
> 1 Life is…
> 2 An aeroplane…
> 3 Friendship…
> 4 A bird of prey…
> 5 A small child…

Fame is a bee.
   It has a song —
It has a sting —
   Ah, too, it has a wing.

Emily Dickinson, *Poem 1763*, date unknown

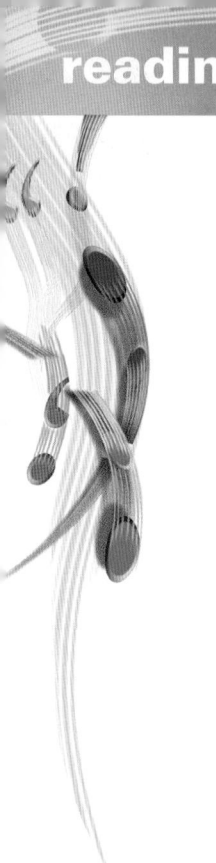

Writing about imagery

The most basic level of writing about images is simply identifying them. In the case of exam texts, such as the poems from different cultures, you may have studied the poems for 2 years — and you have them on the desk in front of you in the exam. You will not pick up many marks simply for saying:

> In verse four of the poem 'Elvis's Twin Sister' there are images to do with religion. There is a rosary and a wimple.

This is typical of a Grade-F/G answer. Once the image has been picked out there is nothing else said about it or done with it.

At Grade C the answer would be focused on the question and a discussion of imagery would probably be part of a broader comment on a subject such as the writer's feelings. A typical response might be:

> In 'Baby-sitting' I can tell that Clarke is nervous about the baby waking up when she writes: '…her nose/Will stream disgustingly…'

So far this answer is around Grade D/E — there is a valid statement and an appropriate quotation.

> This is an unpleasant image and shows that the poet feels uncomfortable.

With the addition of this final sentence the answer becomes a Grade C response because the candidate has shown the link between the image and her statement on the poet's feelings. The image has been identified and there is some comment on the way that the particular image has been used by the poet.

An excellent answer at Grade A might look like this:

> In 'Baby-sitting' the poet manages to make the reader realise just how uncomfortable the character feels looking after someone else's child. The baby with her streaming nose and 'hot midnight rage' seems to be like an alien to the baby-sitter. We can imagine just what 'the perfume of her breath' will be in the case of a small child and this has been chosen to make the reader feel uncomfortable and so share in the character's distress.

Admittedly this is longer than the previous examples — it is difficult to show Grade A qualities in a 1-line answer — but it is not better simply because of its length. The highlighted sections contain key points:

* ✳ '…to make the reader realise…' indicates that the candidate knows the poem was written with a purpose in mind
* ✳ '…uncomfortable the character feels…' shows that the candidate realises that the poem features a character and is not necessarily the poet herself
* ✳ '…seems to be like an alien…' shows a sense of the strangeness that the poet is trying to get across
* ✳ '…this has been chosen…' again indicates that the candidate realises the poet has made a conscious choice

❋ '…and so share…' recognises that the reader becomes involved in the feelings expressed because of the power of the writing

The answer also contains embedded quotations that have been carefully chosen.

Better answers usually contain comment on the way language is used. This might seem hard to achieve at first, but as you work through this section you will find many opportunities to develop your skills in this area.

Task

Each of the following extracts contains a number of images (these are highlighted). For each image, explain what two things are being compared and what effect this is intended to have.

a Bent double like old beggars under sacks,
Knock-kneed, coughing like hags, we cursed through sludge,
Till on the haunting flares we turn our backs,
And towards our distant rest began to trudge.
Men marched asleep. Many had lost their boots,
But limped on, blood-shod. All went lame, all blind;
Drunk with fatigue; deaf even to the hoots
Of gas-shells dropping softly behind.

Wilfred Owen, 'Dulce et Decorum Est', 1918

b Low-shot light of a sharp December
Shifting, lifted a morning haze:
Opening fans of smooth sea-water
Touched in silence the tiny bays:

John Betjeman, 'Beaumaris, December 21, 1963', 1979

c To-morrow, and to-morrow, and to-morrow,
Creeps in this petty pace from day to day
To the last syllable of recorded time,
And all our yesterdays have lighted fools
The way to dusty death. Out, out, brief candle!
Life's but a walking shadow, a poor player
That struts and frets his hour upon the stage
And then is heard no more: it is a tale
Told by an idiot, full of sound and fury,
Signifying nothing.

William Shakespeare, *Macbeth*, 1604

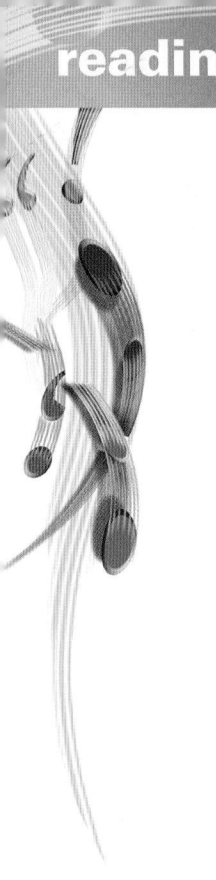

Once you have mastered the skill of interpreting individual images, you need to develop the ability to see what effects a series of images can have. Writers will often use groups of images to make strong suggestions.

Consider the four images below. What genre of film do they suggest?

* a flash of lightning illuminating a dark old house on a hill
* a young couple standing by a broken-down car
* the door to a house being opened by a tall, strange-looking man
* a rocking chair moving by itself

You no doubt came up with the idea that the images are elements of a horror film. Not only that, but you probably formed some idea of the type of horror film — not a vampire or other monster film — maybe a film about a haunted house where something horrible has happened (think of the rocking chair).

You are probably literate with regard to film and television images because you have spent many years absorbing them. Think for a moment how an alien who had never watched television might react to an advert. It would not be clear to such a creature that it was an advert — the alien wouldn't have any concept of what an advert is. For this alien all the moving images in the little box would seem strange and it would take some time before it realised that there were different types of programme.

You might feel a bit like this about poetry. Just as the alien needs to work out how some television programmes differ from others, you need to explore the ways in which poems and poets are different and the ways in which they are the same. A good way to begin to do this is to explore sets of images. Several unpleasant, dark images are obviously intended to unnerve the reader in some way. A set of bright, happy images would have the opposite effect.

Now read the following passage of prose. It is the opening of Dickens's novel *Bleak House* (1853).

Fog everywhere. Fog up the river, where it flows among green aits and meadows; fog down the river, where it rolls defiled among the tiers of shipping and the waterside pollutions of a great (and dirty) city. Fog on the Essex marshes, fog on the Kentish heights. Fog creeping into the cabooses of collier-brigs; fog lying out on the yards, and hovering in the rigging of great ships; fog drooping on the gunwales of barges and small boats. Fog in the eyes and throats of ancient Greenwich pensioners, wheezing by the firesides of their wards; fog in the stem and bowl of the afternoon pipe of the wrathful skipper, down in his close cabin; fog cruelly pinching the toes and fingers of his shivering little 'prentice boy on deck. Chance people on the bridges peeping over the parapets into a nether sky of fog, with fog all round them, as if they were up in a balloon, and hanging in the misty clouds.

There may be some words in the passage that you are not familiar with — aits, gunwale, cabooses — but you can still make sense of it without knowing what all the words mean. In Dickens's London it was common for there to be terrible fogs that mixed with the smoke of thousands of domestic fires to create conditions in which it was hard to breathe.

In trying to understand this passage you should think about the following questions:

* Which word is repeated?
* How many times is it used?
* What might be the reason for this?
* What is the balance of positive and negative connotation?
* What is the writer trying to make you think?
* Why might the writer want you to think this? (In other words, what is the writer's purpose?)

Task

Comment on the imagery Dickens has used and:

a Identify and write down three examples of the use of fog in the passage.

b Say what ideas you think Dickens was trying to get across about London.

c Write down a single adjective that the passage conjures up in your mind.
Give reasons for your comments.

This approach of looking at a group of images can be an effective way to explore a poem. Good comments on imagery could be phrased 'The poet uses positive imagery here in order to…' or 'The poem is full of dark images associated with death. The effect of this is…'

Diction

One sure way to impress the examiner is to make reference to the poet or writer. This shows you recognise that the text was written deliberately.

Diction is the technical term for a writer's choice of words. You could use this term and the phrase 'the writer's choice of words' alternately so that you are not always saying the same thing. There are two main points to consider when you are writing about diction:

* Why has the writer chosen these particular words at this point in the piece?
* What effect do the words have on the reader?

The best answers on poetry always contain clear comments on the poet's intention. You might say things like:

* Here the poet wants to get across the idea that…

* The writer clearly intends to make the reader think about…
* The poet deliberately tries to make the reader feel…

A slight change in wording can affect the sense of a statement. Look at the three examples below:
* You were **asked** to stay away from him.
* You were **advised** to stay away from him.
* You were **ordered** to stay away from him.

Task

Say what effect each of the three statements would have on you. You should think about:
* tone of voice
* what the reasons might be for each statement

It is important that you consider individual words, but you also need to look for patterns of words that are somehow connected. Read the following lines about England from Shakespeare's *Richard II*:

This royal throne of kings, this scept'red isle,
This earth of majesty, this seat of Mars,
This other Eden, demi-paradise,
This fortress built by Nature for herself
Against infection and the hand of war,
This happy breed of men, this little world,
This precious stone set in the silver sea,
Which serves it in the office of a wall,
Or as a moat defensive to a house,
Against the envy of less happier lands;
This blessed plot, this earth, this realm, this England…

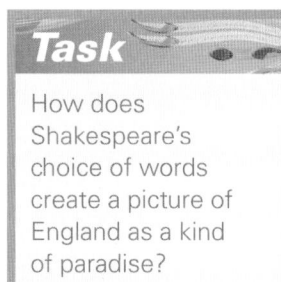

Task

How does Shakespeare's choice of words create a picture of England as a kind of paradise?

A Grade F answer to this task would contain some relevant comment on the text and possibly some listing of images. This is typical of a Grade-F response:

> Shakespeare makes England sound like a good place. He says it is paradise and a precious stone.

The candidate would go on to list more points about England being 'a good place' but would never get beyond the surface of the writing. He would tend to think that Shakespeare is giving his own views on what England was like, as though this were a magazine article promoting England for Elizabethan tourists.

At Grade C the answer would show some awareness of the writer and of the feelings and emotions expressed in the passage. A Grade-C student might typically write:

> The passage is full of strong emotions about England. The writer says that it is a place which is 'This precious stone set in the silver sea' and that it is an 'other

Eden'. It also says it is a 'blessed plot' so the whole passage puts across the idea that England is a good place to live and that it is also a bit like a holy place.

The opening statement shows a grasp of the passage as a whole. It makes a useful generalisation, recognising that the passage is full of 'strong emotions'. Although the candidate does not say specifically what those emotions are, the answer does draw together appropriate details, e.g. 'precious', 'Eden' and 'holy place'. There is also a reference to the writer. It could have been made stronger by commenting that these are not really the writer's views (we have no record of what Shakespeare thought of England). A better student would see that the emotions expressed are those of a particular character in a play.

At Grade A the answer would contain clear comment on the way language is used to achieve particular effects. In the case of this speech, the effect required is to stir the audience into thinking of the greatness of England:

> The whole country is a 'royal throne', a 'scept'red isle' and the 'earth of majesty'. Here the character speaking is suggesting that England is a very important place and this sets up the idea of the country as a perfect land. This idea of perfection is built upon with phrases such as 'other Eden' and 'demi-paradise'. Not only is England a heavenly place to be, it is a strong country described as a 'fortress built by Nature for herself'. This gives a sense of the landscape of the country having been designed to look after its people and to keep them 'Against infection and the hand of war'. Finally, the country is a 'precious stone' and a 'blessed plot'. Throughout the passage the language used to describe England is very positive and at times almost religious. This has the effect of making the reader think of the great things about England and focuses the mind on the country's beauty, strength and importance.

One of the key features of this answer is the way quotations are embedded into the sentences. The quotations are precise and carefully chosen. The answer actually uses some of the same details as the Grade-C answer — 'precious stone', 'other Eden' and 'blessed plot'. But this candidate makes fuller use of the references. One of the ways she achieves this is by showing how they fit into a larger picture, such as 'the idea of perfection'. The candidate also thinks about the effect on the reader. The answer comes to a clear conclusion with three strong ideas summing up the effect of the passage.

A mixture of this embedded quotation technique and the occasional slightly longer quotation (though no more than a couple of lines) is ideal. Use precise quotations that focus on detail and make sure your references are always clear.

To explore the passage from *Richard II* more fully you would of course need to look at the **context** in which it was placed by Shakespeare. It comes from a passionate speech by a faithful old Englishman who is worried about recent changes to what he sees as a great country. Knowing this sheds further light on the feelings that are expressed.

Now apply what you have learnt about diction to answer the tasks given on the passages below. In the first two cases you have been provided with possible openings to the answers at Grade F, Grade C and Grade A. Use some of these openings yourself and try to improve on others so that you begin to see the differences between the three exam grades shown.

> **Remember:** although knowing about the background of a piece of writing can be helpful, be careful not to let yourself give a history lesson or a biography of the writer.

Passage 1

This is an extract from a speech by Mark Antony immediately after the murder of his friend Julius Caesar, from Shakespeare's *Julius Caesar* (1599).

A curse shall light upon the limbs of men:
Domestic fury and fierce civil strife
Shall cumber all the parts of Italy:
Blood and destruction shall be so in use,
And dreadful objects so familiar,
That mothers shall but smile when they behold
Their infants quartered with the hands of war:
All pity choked with custom of fell deeds,
And Caesar's spirit, ranging for revenge,
With Ate by his side come hot from hell,
Shall in these confines, with a monarch's voice,
Cry havoc and let slip the dogs of war…

Task

Comment on the way Mark Antony's anger is brought out through his speech in the above passage.

Grade-F response

Mark Antony is angry because his friend has been killed. He wants destruction for everyone and wants revenge for Caesar.

Grade-C response

The main emotion that Mark Antony has is being angry. He says 'A curse shall light upon the limbs of men' and wants there to be 'Blood and destruction' everywhere.

Grade-A response

Mark Antony's language reflects his obvious anger at the murder of Caesar. He is prepared to bring the whole country to 'blood and destruction' to avenge the death of Caesar.

Passage 2

This is a complete poem by A. E. Housman from *A Shropshire Lad* (1896). The meaning of the poem is not immediately obvious — you have to unpick possible meanings by looking for clues.

Into my heart an air that kills
    From yon far country blows:
What are those blue remembered hills,
   What spires, what farms are those?

That is the land of lost content,
    I see it shining plain,
The happy highways where I went
    And cannot come again.

Task

How does the poet get across his feelings of sadness at the loss of youth?

Grade-F response

The poet says he is sad because he cannot go back to where he was. He remembers the hills but can't visit them again.

Grade-C response

The poet feels sad that he cannot have his past back again. He talks about his past as if it was a place he has visited but is not allowed to go back to: 'The happy highways where I went/And cannot come again.'

Grade-A response

The main emotion expressed in the poem is regret. The poet feels a sense of loss and 'those blue remembered hills' are a symbol of his past life. The whole tone of the language used is of regret.

Passage 3

This is a poem entitled 'The Maldive Shark' by Herman Melville (1888).

About the Shark, phlegmatical one,
Pale sot of the Maldive sea,
The sleek little pilot-fish, azure and slim,
How alert in attendance be.
From his saw-pit of mouth, from his charnel of maw,
They have nothing of harm to dread,
But liquidly glide on his ghastly flank

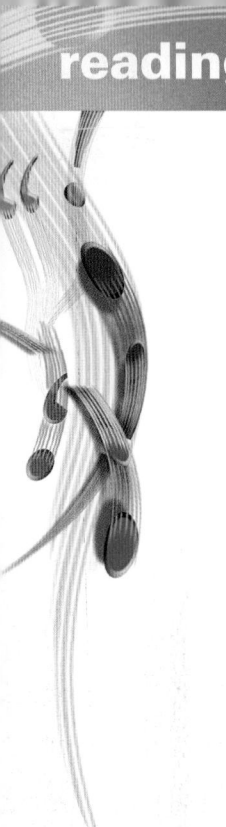

Or before his Gorgonian head;
Or lurk in the port of serrated teeth
In white triple tiers of glittering gates,
And there find a haven when peril's abroad,
And asylum in jaws of the Fates!

They are friends; and friendly they guide him to prey,
Yet never partake of the treat —
Eyes and brains to the dotard lethargic and dull,
Pale ravener of horrible meat.

You will probably not know the meaning of all the words in this poem. There are, however, sufficient words with negative connotations that you can explore before referring to the dictionary. Look at how these words add up to create an overall picture of the shark.

Task

How does the poet suggest to the reader that the Maldive Shark is a foul creature?

Adjectives and adverbs

When you were younger you learned that adjectives and adverbs are describing words. They are not, however, the only means of describing. Using lots of adjectives and adverbs can make a piece of writing — poetry or prose — seem unsophisticated and even childish. Good writers do not rely upon adjectives and adverbs alone; they know that carefully chosen nouns and verbs can carry more weight.

A writer famous for using an economical style is Ernest Hemingway. In the following extract from his novel *The Old Man and the Sea* (1952) an old fisherman has caught the best fish of his life. It is so big that the fish is tied to the side of his small boat. Sharks have picked up the scent and the fisherman is in a desperate race to get the fish to harbour before the sharks eat it.

They came. One turned and went out of sight under the skiff[1] and the old man could feel the skiff shake as he jerked and pulled on the fish. The other watched the old man with his slitted yellow eyes and then came in fast with his half circle of jaws wide to hit the fish where he had already been bitten. The line showed clearly on the top of his brown head and back where the brain joined the spinal cord and the old man drove the knife on the oar into the juncture, withdrew it, and drove it in again into the shark's yellow cat-like eyes. The shark let go of the fish and slid down, swallowing what he had taken as he died.

[1]A skiff is a small fishing boat

There are few adjectives or adverbs in the above passage. Most of the adjectives that are present relate to colours, with the shark's yellow eyes being mentioned twice. The power of the writing comes largely from the direct description of the action.

Task

1 Make a list of the verbs (e.g. 'shake', 'jerked') in the above passage.

2 Write a descriptive paragraph on each of the following subjects, but using no adjectives or adverbs:
   ❋ a sporting contest
   ❋ being caught up in a crowd
   ❋ putting a tent up in the wind

Summary

When commenting on a writer's choice of words you should:
❋ consider what the writer intended to do
❋ say whether the writer has been successful or not
❋ look carefully at the effect a group of words can have
❋ comment on the use of adjectives, adverbs, nouns and verbs (where appropriate)
❋ consider the effect that the full piece of writing might have on the reader
❋ remember to make a comment about purpose and audience

Now put what you have learned into practice.

Task

How do the words used in the poem below create a picture of Timothy Winters?

Timothy Winters comes to school
With eyes as wide as a football-pool,
Ears like bombs and teeth like splinters:
A blitz of a boy is Timothy Winters.

His belly is white, his neck is dark,
And his hair is an exclamation-mark.
His clothes are enough to scare a crow
And through his britches the blue winds blow.

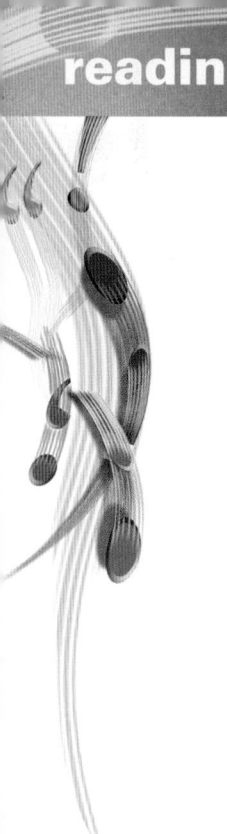

When teacher talks he won't hear a word
And he shoots down dead the arithmetic-bird,
He licks the pattern off his plate
And he's not even heard of the Welfare State.

Timothy Winters has bloody feet
And he lives in a house on Suez Street,
He sleeps in a sack on the kitchen floor
And they say there aren't boys like him anymore.

Old Man Winters likes his beer
And his missus ran off with a bombardier,
Grandma sits in the grate with a gin
And Timothy's dosed with an aspirin.

The welfare Worker lies awake
But the law's as tricky as a ten-foot snake,
So Timothy Winters drinks his cup
And slowly goes on growing up.

At Morning Prayers the Master helves
for children less fortunate than ourselves,
And the loudest response in the room is when
Timothy Winters roars 'Amen!'

So come one angel, come on ten
Timothy Winters says 'Amen
Amen amen amen amen.'
Timothy Winters, Lord. Amen

Charles Causley, 'Timothy Winters', 1957

Lines

How do you recognise a poem? The most obvious answer is that it is written in lines. This simple fact can control the way in which you grasp its sense.

You are often asked to write about the layout of a poem on the page. Rather than just saying that the poem is 'thin' or 'fat', it is much more useful to address the fact that it is written in lines. Look at the following sentence:

Chipped china mugs, the radio on, fried egg sandwiches dripping gold down old men's chins, each person is an island in this steamed up sea of warmth and noise.

This is in fact part of a poem. When you see the same words arranged into lines you might think about particular words in a different way because of their position on the line. Some ideas become thoughts in themselves, such as 'the radio on'.

Chipped china mugs
the radio on
fried egg sandwiches
dripping gold
down old men's chins
each person is
an island in this
steamed up sea
of warmth and noise.
No one bothers
to take their jacket
off. No one
likes to stay that
long. They're only
here for the chat you
see they're here
to fill themselves
with a sense of
camaraderie
before going
home to their lives.

Task

Comment on the way that the layout of the poem affects your reading of it.

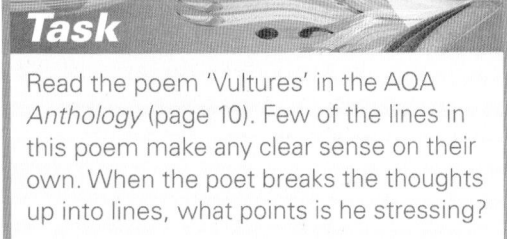

Task

Read the poem 'Vultures' in the AQA *Anthology* (page 10). Few of the lines in this poem make any clear sense on their own. When the poet breaks the thoughts up into lines, what points is he stressing?

Rhythm

One important example of how poets use language to achieve an effect is rhythm. If you can recognise rhythm and say something about the way it affects your reading of a poem, then you will pick up marks in the examination. This applies to:

❋ English Paper 2 Section B — poems from different cultures
❋ English Literature Section B — pre- and post-1914 poetry

Rhythm particularly appears in poetry and some verse writing in plays, such as those by Shakespeare. Ordinary English speech does have rhythm — 'I like to be in England and I like to be in Spain but I'd really rather be in Alicante' — but you may not notice its patterns. Poets often exaggerate and build up the patterns of stresses that appear in everyday speech to create definite rhythms. Take the word 'yesterday'. Say it aloud a few times in succession. You will soon spot that some parts of the word are stressed while others are skipped over quickly and are unstressed. The word breaks down as follows (S = stressed; U = unstressed):

```
 S    U    S
Yes  ter  day
```

You might be more familiar with the use of rhythm in music. Take the obvious example of rap music — it consists of patterns of syllables that have been arranged to create a beat.

Writing that consists of a definite arrangement of syllables in order to create rhythm is called **verse**. One of the key features of verse you will need to learn how to identify is the rhythm itself. If a poem has an up-beat, happy rhythm, it might well be because the subject matter of the poem is also pleasant.

Task

Mark the stresses in the following words and phrases:

* international
* conference
* antique
* antiquated
* She walks in beauty like the night
* Such life here through lengths of hours
* Father, father, where are you going?
* Miniver Cheevy, child of scorn

Of course, you might encounter poetry that deliberately turns this idea on its head. Take the example of the poem 'Porphyria's Lover' (1834) by Robert Browning. Read the extract quoted below; at this point in the poem the lover strangles Porphyria with her own hair. Look closely at the conversation he has with himself here (the entire poem is a **dramatic monologue**):

>   I found
> A thing to do, and all her hair
> In one long yellow string I wound
> Three times her little throat around,
> And strangled her.

The moment is all the more horrific because the killer carries on talking as though nothing has happened. Try to read this aloud as though it is a piece of natural speech — you will find that something unusual happens around the words 'yellow string'. Here the tone changes and becomes dark.

You might have studied the two Robert Browning poems in the AQA *Anthology*, 'My Last Duchess' and 'The Laboratory'. These poems also feature characters whose insane jealousy is revealed only through the manner of their speech. An important part of the speech of these characters is the rhythm that Browning uses.

Note that rhythm is an essential part of a poem, so make sure you do not simply write 'the poet uses rhythm' as though it was added as an afterthought.

A well-known example of the use of rhythm can be found in the poem 'Night Mail' by W. H. Auden. This poem was written specially for the Post Office's 1936 promotional film about the trains that carried the mail all over the country. The mail was sorted on board while the train ran through the night. Here are two extracts from the poem:

This is the Night Mail crossing the border,
Bringing the cheque and the postal order,
Letters for the rich, letters for the poor,
The shop at the corner and the girl next door.
[...]
News circumstantial, news financial,
Letters with holiday snaps to enlarge in,
Letters with faces scrawled in the margin,
Letters from uncles, cousins, and aunts,
Letters to Scotland from the South of France,
Letters of condolence to Highlands and Lowlands
Notes from overseas to Hebrides
Written on paper of every hue,
The pink, the violet, the white and the blue,
The chatty, the catty, the boring, adoring,
The cold and official and the heart's outpouring,
Clever, stupid, short and long,
The typed and the printed and the spelt all wrong.

Task

Read the poem aloud to yourself and then mark where the stresses are.

You will probably have picked up straight-away that the poem was written to echo the sound of a train running along the track.

Examples of student performance

Consider the following question:

What poetic devices has the poet used in 'Night Mail' to make the poem entertaining?

An examiner might expect to see the following in response to such a task:

Grade A detailed comment about a few carefully selected techniques	
Grade C picks out many different techniques but only says a little about each one	
Grade F many simple points, probably written as a list	

Task

Read the three beginnings to answers below and then put them into the right grade order, from lowest to highest. One answer is Grade F, one is Grade C and one is Grade A.

Answer 1

Auden sets out to create the sense of a moving train through the use of rhythm in 'Night Mail'. The sound that is made when the poem is read aloud mirrors the sound of a train moving on the track — it even changes occasionally to suggest that the motion is not exactly regular. In addition we are presented with a list of the types of things that the train is carrying. This set of items contains a good deal of repetition — the word 'Letters' for example. This is part of the rhythm and also reinforces the idea that the journey is repetitive.

Answer 2

The poet has told us what is on the train. There are letters from uncles and letters to Scotland and they are on different coloured paper. The words sound a bit like a train. Some words are used again. The words rhyme. There are letters for poor people and rich people and the train is crossing the border. It is called the Night Mail and it used to go up and down the country at night with letters that had been put in the post.

Answer 3

The poem has a rhythm that sounds like the rhythm of a train. It uses rhyme at the end of every two lines. This makes it better to read. The poet tells us what is on the train and goes into detail about the types of letter that the train has on it. Sometimes the words sound a bit different and this is because the train sounds different when it goes over different bits of track. The poet spends a lot of time talking about letters and this says that the train is always making the same journey.

Task

1 Take some of the main ideas from the Grade-F and Grade-C answers and use these, plus your own thoughts, to write your own answer to the question.

2 Use the Grade-A answer as a start for an answer of your own. (You might want to add a quotation or two to the Grade-A answer first.)

One important point to note about writing about poetry in the exam is that **you cannot say everything**. Be **selective** and focus on what you **understand**. It is better to say a lot about a little than a little about a lot.

Style

All writers have to make a choice about how to write down their ideas — in other words, which style to use. Style is difficult to define. A useful comment on style was made by the poet Robert Frost: 'All the fun's in how you say a thing.'

Students often make the mistake of thinking that a piece of writing could only ever have been written in one particular way. To do well you need to be able to:

❋ recognise that a text has been written in a certain style for a reason
❋ comment on the effect that style has on the reader

Even the simplest of ideas can be expressed in a variety of styles. The following three statements give basically the same information but they are written in different styles (you could say different **registers** are used):

❋ My husband's employers have terminated his contract.
❋ My husband's been sacked.
❋ My old man's been given the boot.

The first statement is formal to the extent that it sounds cold and impersonal. The second one is direct and neutral. The third is chatty, colloquial and possibly emotional.

You should recognise that different writers can have different styles, for example formal, colloquial, humorous and so on. *Lord of the Flies* is written in a different style from *Catcher in the Rye*, which is in turn different in style from *To Kill a Mockingbird* (even though the last two novels are both first person narratives).

Task

Read the two passages below. Both are about Liverpool. Comment on the ways in which the style of each passage affects your appreciation and enjoyment of what is being said.

1

Liverpool's culture and heritage

Liverpool has more museums and art galleries than any other UK city outside London. But to explore each of them is just to scratch the surface of the City's rich vein of artistic and cultural attractions.

The city and its surrounding area also boast some of the most impressive and spectacular architecture in Europe. From the splendid scale of St George's Hall to the imposing presence of the city's two cathedrals, Liverpool is blessed with fine

buildings — public and private. And this wonderful legacy from past generations is not confined to the city centre. Elsewhere, in places like Birkenhead's Hamilton Square and Port Sunlight Village in the Wirral, are fine examples of Merseyside's rich heritage.

2

I took a train to Liverpool. They were having a festival of litter when I arrived. Citizens had taken time off from their busy activities to add crisp packets, empty cigarette boxes, and carrier-bags to the otherwise bland and neglected landscape. They fluttered gaily in the bushes and brought colour and texture to pavements and gutters. And to think that elsewhere we stick these objects in rubbish bags.

In another bout of extravagant madness, I had booked a room in the Adelphi Hotel. I had seen it from the street on earlier visits and it appeared to have an old-fashioned grandeur about it that I was keen to investigate. On the other hand, it looked expensive and I wasn't sure my trousers could stand another session in the trouser press. So I was most agreeably surprised when I checked in to discover that I was entitled to a special weekend rate and that there would be money spare for a nice meal and a parade of beer in any of the many wonderful pubs in which Liverpool specializes.

And so, soon afterwards, I found myself, like all fresh arrivals in Liverpool, in the grand and splendourous surroundings of the Philharmonic, clutching a pint glass and rubbing shoulders with a happy Friday-evening throng. The Phil (you can call it this if you have been there twice) was in fact a bit too crowded for my liking.

Bill Bryson, *Notes from a Small Island*, 1995

Your own language

When you are writing about literature you will use language in a more controlled manner than you would in everyday speech. You are asked to make judgements about works of literature, and these should be considered and supported by evidence from the text.

Avoid writing simplistic statements (e.g. 'I like this poem'; 'This book is good'). Instead, use language such as:

* This line has the effect of...
* The poet tries to make the reader feel...
* The writer has been successful in his attempt to...
* One effect of the poem is to make the reader think about...

Don't make sweeping statements (e.g. 'This book is brilliant'; 'She is the greatest poet in the English language'). Instead, practise using phrases such as:

* The power of this piece of writing comes from...
* The poet's skill allows her to...
* The poem is effective because...

You can create combinations of words and phrases useful for commenting on literature by making a table such as the one below. You could use phrases from the left-hand column with some from the right-hand column (with a few joining words). You might want to add to this, or make your own version of the table.

the writer	conveys a sense of
in his/her attempt to	express the feeling that
the poet is most convincing when	creates the effect of
this is successful as	is powerful because
to try to persuade the reader	deliberately leads the reader to think that

Whether or not you like the text has no real bearing on your ability to comment on it as a piece of literature. You need to comment on how **effective** the text is, but do not fall into the trap of saying whether or not you like it. You are a student of literature, not simply an audience for the writer.

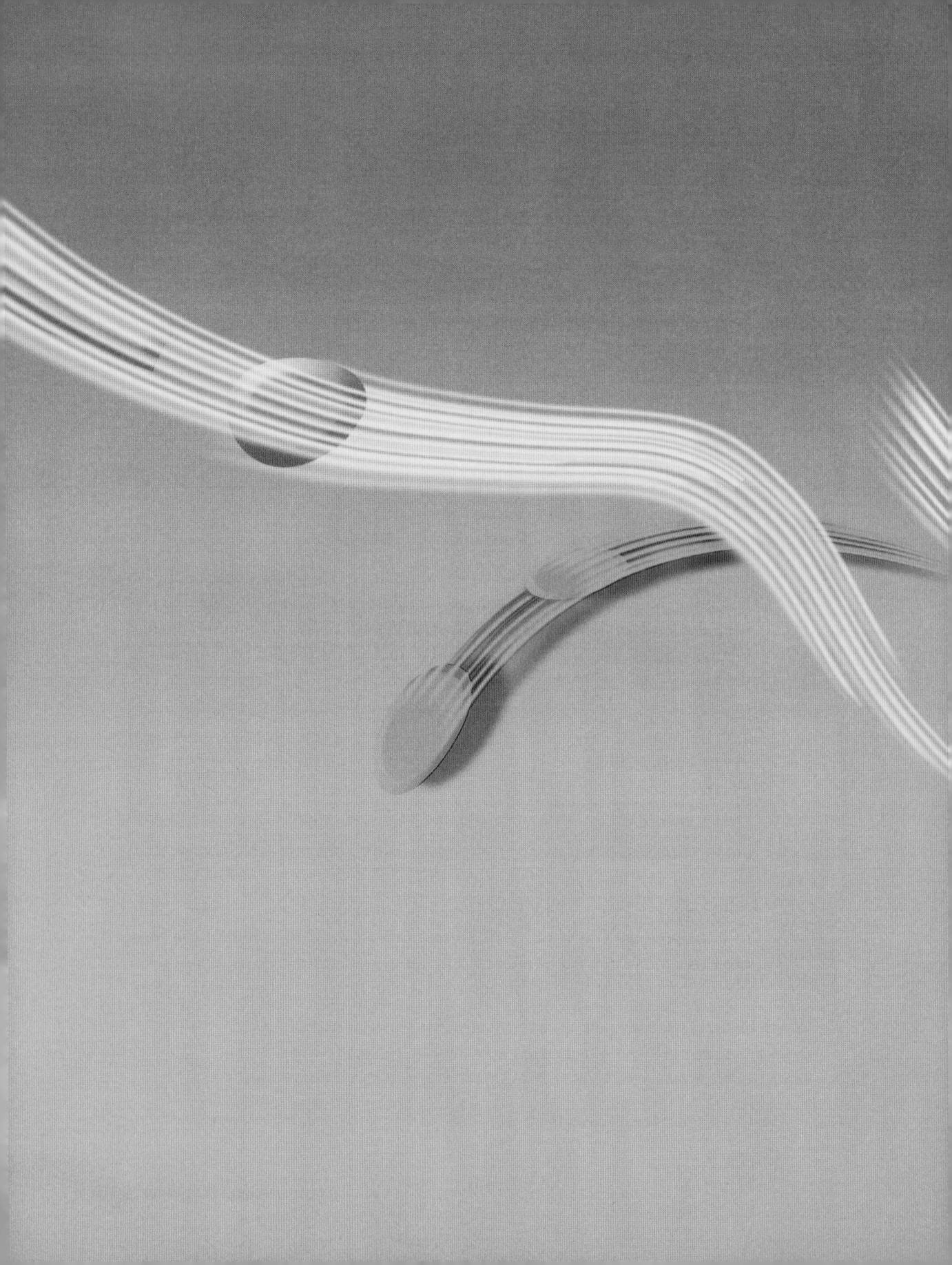

Section

2

Writing

Rules, forms, purpose and audience

Can you imagine a world in which nobody needed to write? You may think you don't like writing and prefer to leave it to the professionals, but you might be surprised at how much writing you actually do, even leaving aside what your teachers make you do. The fact is that almost everyone, in our society at least, has to engage in some form of writing, even if it amounts to no more than filling in a form or sending a Valentine's card.

Of course, you probably do a lot more than that. It's more than likely that you regularly send text messages or e-mails and you may contribute to message boards or chat rooms. In fact, modern communications, and the internet in particular, have expanded hugely the amount of writing that people do.

Here are some figures for the number of entries thrown up by a search engine:

Emmerdale	214,000	*Coronation Street*	413,000
EastEnders	680,000	David Beckham	1,680,000
Harry Potter	12,400,000	Shakespeare	14,800,000
Big Brother	18,300,000		

If we assume a modest 100 words per entry (and it's likely to be much more), that's around 5 billion words. What's more, it's probably fair to say that a large proportion of those 5 billion words were written not by professionals, but by ordinary people. When George Orwell invented the phrase 'Big Brother' in his novel *Nineteen Eighty-Four*, which he wrote in 1948, he could not have imagined that his words would have produced more on-line writing than the works of Shakespeare, even if most of it has nothing to do with his original story.

Three rules for writing

No matter what you are writing, whether it is a leaflet advertising a new rock group or a scientific article on the gastropods of southeast England, there are three golden rules that *always* apply:

Note: always think about **purpose** and **audience** when you write.

1 You must have something to write about.

2 You must have a reason for writing.

3 You must put yourself in the position of your reader.

The first rule may seem so obvious as to not be worth mentioning. After all, it is impossible to write about gastropods without a lot of detailed knowledge. But students frequently do not think enough about their subject before starting to write. Even if you are making it up, you must 'know' your subject.

Look at this student's poor attempt to write a piece of science fiction:

> I woke up and it was sunny. I had my breakfast and set out on my paper round. As I passed the field, I noticed a shiny object in the sky. It was a flying saucer. It landed in the field and as I watched, it opened. These slimy things came out. They were green and had tentacles on. They were aliens and they sent out killer rays. I was frightened so I ran away. Later I learned they had caught some of my friends and taken them up to brainwash them with lasers and needles.

It is plain that this is unconvincing, although the spelling, grammar and punctuation are perfectly accurate. The question is, why doesn't it succeed?

Task

Write down as many reasons as you can to explain why this piece of writing would not make the bestseller list.

Let's consider this science fiction attempt against the three rules for writing in turn:

* First, the writer has not thought about the subject. The piece is full of off-the-shelf ideas taken from every bad science fiction film about alien invasions you can think of. Aliens arrive in flying saucers; they are always slimy; they have tentacles and so on. Why? Because that's what you see in the films. It is impossible to be entirely original but you must at least try to avoid the obvious.

* Second, even in this short paragraph there doesn't seem to be any purpose or direction to the writing. It is a set of random thoughts. What is the point of the sunny day or breakfast? Is the writer trying to surprise or amaze

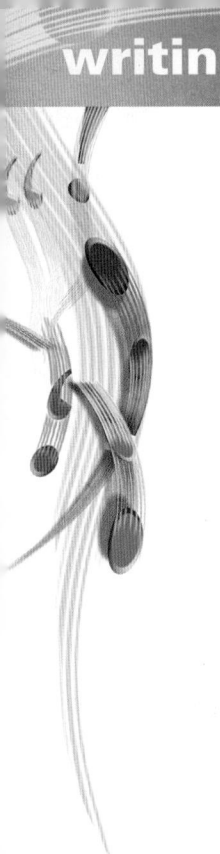

us? If this is the introduction to a longer story, what exactly is supposed to lead us to new developments?

✳ Third, the candidate has not read the piece from the reader's point of view. It is matter-of-fact, with no sense of tension. If you really encountered a flying saucer, would you simply 'notice' it? You would at least gaze in disbelief. Even if you have good, vivid ideas, it is not enough simply to hold them in your head. You must show the reader what you see in your mind's eye through the words you use.

Now look at a piece of fiction written over a century ago, which describes a similar situation. It is an extract from *The War of the Worlds* by H. G. Wells, first published in 1898.

When I returned to the common the sun was setting. Scattered groups were hurrying from the direction of Woking, and one or two persons were returning. The crowd about the pit had increased, and stood out black against the lemon yellow of the sky — a couple of hundred people, perhaps. There were raised voices, and some sort of struggle appeared to be going on about the pit. Strange imaginings passed through my mind. As I drew nearer I heard Stent's voice:

'Keep back! Keep back!'

A boy came running towards me.

'It's a-movin',' he said to me as he passed; 'a-screwin' and a-screwin' out. I don't like it. I'm a-goin' 'ome, I am.'

I saw a young man, a shop assistant in Woking I believe he was, standing on the cylinder and trying to scramble out of the hole again. The crowd had pushed him in. The end of the cylinder was being screwed out from within. Nearly two feet of shining screw projected. Somebody blundered against me, and I narrowly missed being pitched onto the top of the screw. I turned, and as I did so the screw must have come out, for the lid of the cylinder fell upon the gravel with a ringing concussion. I stuck my elbow into the person behind me, and turned my head towards the Thing again. For a moment that circular cavity seemed perfectly black. I had the sunset in my eyes.

I think everyone expected to see a man emerge — possibly something a little unlike us terrestrial men, but in all essentials a man. I know I did. But, looking, I presently saw something stirring within the shadow: greyish billowy movements, one above another, and then two luminous disks — like eyes. Then something resembling a little grey snake, about the thickness of a walking stick, coiled up out of the writhing middle, and wriggled in the air towards me — and then another.

I stood petrified and staring. A big greyish rounded bulk, the size, perhaps, of a bear, was rising slowly and painfully out of the cylinder. As it bulged up and caught the light, it glistened like wet leather.

3

Two large dark-coloured eyes were regarding me steadfastly. The mass that framed them, the head of the thing, was rounded, and had, one might say, a face. There was a mouth under the eyes, the lipless brim of which quivered and panted, and dropped saliva. The whole creature heaved and pulsated convulsively. A lank tentacular appendage gripped the edge of the cylinder, another swayed in the air.

Those who have never seen a living Martian can scarcely imagine the strange horror of its appearance. Even at this first encounter, this first glimpse, I was overcome with disgust and dread.

Kobal

A Martian in the 1953 film of *The War of the Worlds*

The passage is obviously longer, but it covers roughly the same ground as the candidate's piece. However, what is remarkable is that when H. G. Wells wrote *The War of the Worlds* there was nothing on which he could base his ideas. There were no equivalents of *Star Wars* or *Star Trek* to borrow from. As a result, he had to invent everything about the aliens but make them seem as vivid as if he was writing about a subject familiar to everybody. In other words, he had to create the illusion of *real* facts about the invasion. Notice how Wells provides a named setting — a common near Woking — rather than a vague place. He introduces ordinary people and describes how they react, and provides detailed 'facts' about the gradually opening cylinder and the emerging creature.

Wells has a clear purpose, which is to amaze and convey a sense of horror and threat. As we might expect of something written so long ago, the writing seems a little old-fashioned, but we can see clearly how the writer keeps his eye on his audience ('Those who have never seen a living Martian can scarcely imagine the strange horror of its appearance'). That he appears to struggle to describe the horror makes it seem more real.

A tribute to H. G. Wells's skill occurred 40 years later, when the famous director Orson Welles created a radio broadcast of *The War of the Worlds,* which convinced millions of Americans that a Martian invasion was actually taking place.

You will probably not want to write much in the way of fantasy or science fiction for your GCSE, but thinking hard and in sufficient detail is vital, whatever your subject. Here are a couple of tasks to exercise your mind.

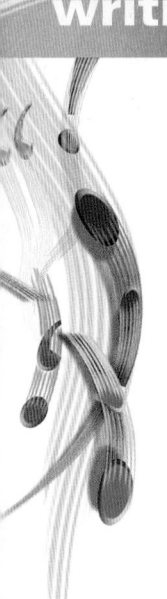

Forms of writing

There are two broad categories of writing:

1 Writing that in some way concerns **factual** information. The range is enormous and may include anything from philosophy to fanzines. To attempt this sort of writing you must have a clear grasp of facts and ideas.

2 Writing that is essentially **fictional** (sometimes called original writing). Novels, short stories, plays and poetry all fall into this category. Writing of this sort may involve a high level of invention, as in the case of the passage from *The War of the Worlds*, or relate closely to real-life experience and situations.

A list of forms of writing would be endless, but here are some common ones:

* lifestyle magazine
* fairy story
* car review
* romantic novel
* men's magazine
* television guide
* history book
* travel guide
* autobiography
* scientific journal
* cookery book
* short story

Purpose and audience

All communication has a **purpose**. Even a single word may have a purpose, such as a sign on a shop door saying 'closed'. Normally, you do not consider the purpose of your communication. If you meet a friend in the street, you probably do not plan what you are going to say. If, however, you had to give your friend some bad news, you would think harder about what to say and how to say it.

In the case of writing, certain subjects have a particular kind of language associated with them. Look at a geography or history textbook and you will see specialist language. You would expect the text to be written in a formal way — you would be surprised if the tone was chatty and informal. On the

other hand, it would be unusual to write a mobile phone text message in a formal way.

The purpose of a piece of writing is linked closely to the **audience** for which it is written. In ordinary conversation the audience is usually in front of you. If you know your audience well, you will instinctively choose the right words for your purpose and, if necessary, adapt to the audience's reaction. You need to develop a similar sense of your audience in written communication. When you are writing, however, the audience is usually invisible or unknown to you. Although you may first think of your teacher or the examiner as the audience, this is not really the case. You will never be set the task of writing to your teacher or to the examiner. They will, of course, read your work, but your writing might have to be in any one of a number of styles. For example, if you were asked to write in the style of an article for a popular newspaper, your audience might be a typical *Sun* reader.

Always ask yourself the question, '**Who is this for?**' Think about your audience and consider how it will respond to your words:

❋ Will the audience understand?

❋ Have you struck the right note?

❋ Is it the kind of information the audience would expect to read?

Task

Read passages 1 and 2 that follow and say what kind of audience you think each was written for and why.

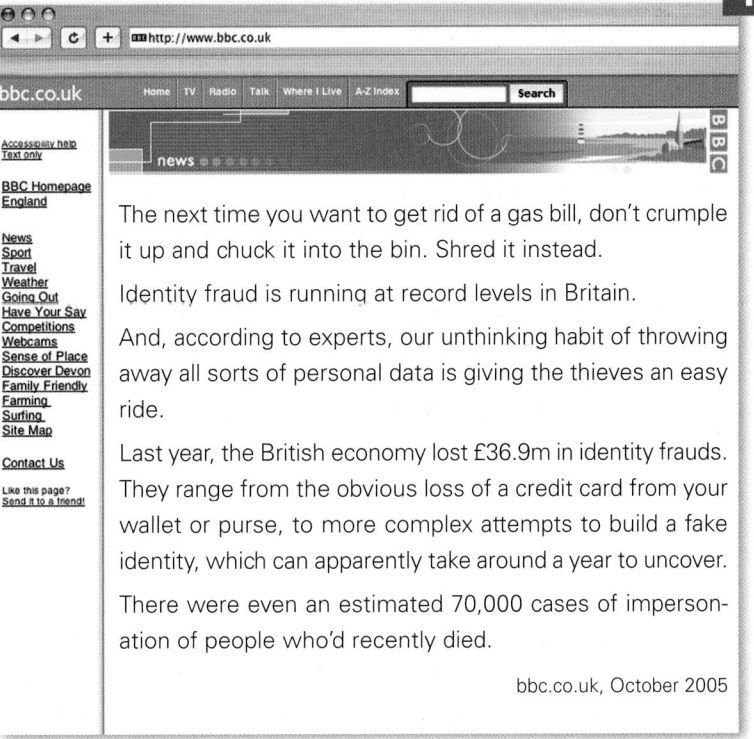

The next time you want to get rid of a gas bill, don't crumple it up and chuck it into the bin. Shred it instead.

Identity fraud is running at record levels in Britain.

And, according to experts, our unthinking habit of throwing away all sorts of personal data is giving the thieves an easy ride.

Last year, the British economy lost £36.9m in identity frauds. They range from the obvious loss of a credit card from your wallet or purse, to more complex attempts to build a fake identity, which can apparently take around a year to uncover.

There were even an estimated 70,000 cases of impersonation of people who'd recently died.

bbc.co.uk, October 2005

2

Whatever you do today, you are leaving a blatant trail of information behind you. It is personal, sensitive information, and it is easily abused. Everything you do to live will create this data trail. You might be dumping receipts for plastic purchases; you might be banking or shopping online — or possibly all you do is bank or shop with an organisation, so that now it has a database with you on it. You might have just chucked an old utility bill into the bin, or maybe you forgot to redirect your mail from your last address, or opened a store card or catalogue account years ago and didn't cancel it. You're just living in the easy-access, modern commodity world. Everyone you know is living like this, it seems normal, so it has to be OK.

Guardian, 25 October 2003

Task

At the age of 18 you may be contacted by banks and credit card companies trying to persuade you to open accounts with them.

Using the information from the two articles above, write the text of a leaflet explaining the dangers of identity fraud to young people and advising them how to protect themselves against it.

Sometimes the nature of the audience will not be clear. For example, if you choose the 'write to describe' task on Paper 2 Section B, you may not have any information about the audience. In such cases you have a choice: you can either make up your own audience or you can assume that the audience is a reasonably intelligent, interested adult, such as your teacher or examiner!

A typical audience for one of the examination writing tasks on English Paper 1 Section B might be:

* your headteacher
* a local MP
* a friend

* the local council
* parents
* a local newspaper

On English Paper 2 Section B the writing to inform question and the writing to explain question often give you an audience such as those listed above. The writing to describe question tends to have an open, unstated audience.

Your writing needs to be slightly different for each audience. You would not use the same kind of language in a formal letter to your local MP as you would if you were trying to persuade a friend.

How your writing is assessed

Chapter 4

Your writing will be assessed using three **Assessment Objectives (AOs)**:

AO3(i)	Communicate clearly and imaginatively, using and adapting forms for different readers and purposes.
AO3(ii)	Organise ideas into sentences, paragraphs and whole texts using a variety of linguistic and structural features.
AO3(iii)	Use a range of sentence structures effectively with accurate punctuation and spelling.

Your writing is assessed on four separate occasions against the same three AOs.

There is more on each of the types of writing in Section 3 of this book.

Where you are assessed	Type of writing
Coursework — Media	analyse, review, comment
Coursework — Original Writing	explore, imagine, entertain
Paper 1 Section B	argue, persuade, advise
Paper 2 Section B	inform, explain, describe

Although the three AOs for writing appear separately above, in reality they are often combined. You could not communicate clearly without being able to use sentences properly, for example. To help you become familiar with the AOs for writing, however, they are covered in this chapter individually.

AO3(i)

Communicate clearly and imaginatively, using and adapting forms for different readers and purposes

Key words	What the key words mean
communicate clearly	Your writing is well organised so that the reader (your teacher or an examiner) can see what it is you are trying to get across.
communicate imaginatively	You try to take a different approach from that which other people might take. This means you have to stand back from the task and think about the impression you want to give of yourself. If you can find a different or unusual approach, then this might create a good impression.

Key words	What the key words mean
using and adapting forms	This refers to forms of writing. You need to know, for example, what form a film review takes before you attempt to write one yourself. Most film reviews are written in around 1,000 words because they are to appear in newspapers or magazines. You will have to adapt the form to write a substantial review. Each time you write in a chosen form you should think about how you can best adapt the form to suit the task you have been set.
for different readers and purposes	The idea of purpose and audience is stressed throughout this book. It is vital that you take into account the audience you are writing for. There is a big difference in approach between writing formally to your local MP and writing to advise one of your friends. You need to show you can change your style to match the audience.

Before you think about your own writing it is a good idea to look at examples by other people to give you some ideas. You should be able to adapt the material given into another form. Thinking carefully about the likely audience for a piece of writing is one of the keys to its success.

Task

Look at the leaflet reproduced below. It is concerned with health. Other than for Paper 1 Section B of the exam, it is unlikely that you will be asked to produce a leaflet. Much of the impact of leaflets comes from their design. This is done by professional graphic designers and is not a skill you need to develop in order to do well at GCSE English.

Using information from the leaflet and your own knowledge, adapt the material in one of the following ways:

1 Write an essay on the subject of the need for exercise and healthy eating as part of a modern lifestyle.

2 Write the introduction to a website called **www.youandyourhealth-matters.com**.

3 Write an article for a teenage magazine persuading teenagers to adopt a healthy lifestyle.

Weight

Being overweight — the problems

Being excessively overweight should be taken seriously.

Next time you are in a supermarket, pick up a standard 1 kg bag of sugar and weigh it in your hands. Many people are 2 stones overweight — try to imagine having to carry 13 bags around all day, everyday. You can see why being overweight can quite literally wear the body out.

Your heart has to work harder as your weight increases. As well as having more fat on their bodies, overweight people often have more fat in their blood, which can lead to a build-up of deposits in blood vessels and increase the risk of strokes and heart attacks.

Joints can also suffer. Your body is designed to carry a certain weight. Just as car springs will groan or snap with an overloaded boot, so joints will complain if asked to carry too much. In the long term, you could suffer from arthritis. Correct your weight and your joints will reward you with increased mobility. Many people who lose weight find their ease of movement increases dramatically.

There are many other health risks from being excessively overweight — high blood pressure, strokes, diabetes, bronchitis and gallstones. But remember, the risk of suffering these complaints can fall dramatically if you get nearer to your ideal weight.

Why do people put on weight?

Many believe that being overweight is a 'glandular' disturbance, but this is very rare. The truth is much simpler. You put on weight when energy intake exceeds energy output — when you eat and drink more than your body can use in your everyday activities.

People often assume that their emotional problems are the result of being overweight. This is sometimes true, but the opposite is more usual. Becoming excessively fat, or too thin, can be a way of expressing pent-up anger. If you are eating because you are anxious, insecure, lonely, depressed or tense, once these stresses are reduced, weight loss often becomes much easier.

Whatever you do…

Don't turn to crash diets, appetite suppressants, or any other fads, as these are only effective in the short term and before long any weight loss will soon reappear. Your aim is to rework your lifestyle and eating and drinking habits…think long term, rather than short term. Your new food choices are for life and your shopping habits should change with them.

When you've succeeded

Once your weight is right and you've made new food choices to help maintain a healthy weight, you'll look trimmer and feel better. Your risk of serious illness will have been reduced along with the reading on the weighing scales. Your extra confidence and energy will have you wanting to improve in other areas of your life. Soon you will be taking on challenges that you would not have dreamt of before!

What you can do

Food

1 Eat three moderate meals a day rather than one large one and remember it's the type of foods you eat that are important, not just the quantity.

2 Choose low-fat foods — grilled, steamed or poached — and eat less fatty fried foods, such as chips, which should be kept for an occasional treat.

3 Use all fats, oils, spreads, margarines and butters as sparingly as possible. Choose a low-fat spread and make sure it's high in polyunsaturates.

4 Eat plenty of fresh vegetables and salads and choose fresh fruit instead of pudding.

5 Fibre-rich starchy foods, like wholemeal bread, pasta, jacket potatoes and high-fibre breakfast cereals, should be included in your diet as they help to satisfy your appetite without providing too many calories.

6 Drink plenty of fluids like water and low-calorie soft drinks, and cut down on alcohol, which is high in calories.

7 Avoid sugar, sweets, crisps, cakes, biscuits, pastries and pies, as these are all high in calories.

Exercise

1 The other side of balancing the weight equation is regular, brisk exercise, such as walking or swimming. It will help shed pounds and tune up the body's weight regulation system.

2 Use the stairs, not the lift. Say 'no' to a short bus or car ride — walk. Try a few sports to find one you enjoy.

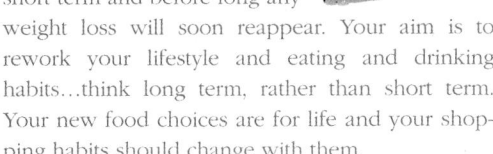

Dieting myths

There is a common misunderstanding that weight control can be accomplished overnight. Not surprising, with so many 'wonder diets' around.

Losing excess weight is a gradual process. You should aim to lose about 1–2 lbs per week until you reach a weight which is ideal for your height and build. The most effective way to lose weight is by modifying your diet and taking regular exercise. To lose weight you need to take in less energy (calories) than you burn up.

Many people think that to lose weight the sugar in their diet is the only thing that should be reduced. However, it is more important to reduce the amount of fat that you eat, while remembering that some fat is essential for good health so it should not be cut out altogether.

Being excessively overweight is not just a cosmetic problem — your health will suffer if you keep your weight higher than is ideal for you. Once you have reached your ideal weight your should continue to exercise and eat a well-balanced diet to maintain your ideal weight.

Risk factors — the big 6

Remember that being overweight is one of several factors causing heart disease — there are five others to bear in mind.

Help your heart by making healthier choices
Excess weight puts strain on your heart
Avoid high blood pressure
Relax and reduce your stress levels
Take regular exercise
You should try to give up smoking

As a start, collect all six leaflets in this series and act today to give your heart a healthy boost. Look after it and it will look after you.

Extracts from a leaflet by the Flora Institute Project, reproduced with kind permission of *Unilever*

AO3(ii)

Organise ideas into sentences, paragraphs and whole texts using a variety of linguistic and structural features

Key words	What the key words mean
organise ideas into sentences, paragraphs and whole texts	You must convince the reader that you have deliberately organised your writing. Sentences should be correctly formed and flow logically from one into another. Paragraphs should exist for definite reasons, not simply appear every 8 lines to make the page look pretty. A whole piece of writing should have a clear structure.
using a variety of linguistic and structural features	These might include techniques such as: ✱ using a short sentence for effect ✱ employing the rule of three to emphasise a point (see page 118) ✱ asking rhetorical questions ✱ using discourse markers ✱ using a 1-line paragraph to attract attention

Again, it is helpful to look at a piece of writing such as the article on pages 85–87 to see how a professional writer might achieve the skills assessed in AO3(ii). (Bear in mind that the article was not written for a GCSE course.) By looking closely at the way that a writer approaches a particular subject, you can learn some of the tricks yourself.

Illustrations: John Richardson

Reveal your super self!

Learning to break free of others' demands and to meet your own needs is key to achieving whatever you want from life, says psychotherapist **Anne Nicholls**. It's time to put yourself first for once — you'll be amazed at the power you can generate from a little word like 'no'!

What would you do with a small cash windfall? Buy yourself something new to wear? Or would you spend it all on the family because you felt guilty about treating yourself? If so, you're not alone. Many people feel they have to please others at their own expense, and it's not just about money. People who say yes to every demand on their time and energies; parents who can't bring themselves to say no to their children; workers who let others take advantage of them — they are all showing signs of an inability to 'please themselves'.

So what? you might say. It's good to do things for other people. But as with all good things, it's possible to overdo it — and there can be unpleasant side effects. Being known as the person who'll do anything for anyone is fine up to a point. But without realising it, you could find yourself being drawn into the selflessness trap. It starts when you begin to feel unappreciated, and then guilty if you allow your resentment to show. Frustration can

set in, leading to despair, and feeling that you're stuck because you can't possibly do anything differently.

The problem is that people who give their all to others have nothing left over for themselves. Losing sight of their needs and feelings, they become reluctant or even afraid to ask for what they want. They find that they no longer have the time, the confidence or the energy to achieve their own goals.

So why do people martyr themselves? The heart of it is a low sense of self-worth. People who believe that their only value lies in what they can do for everyone else tend to try to 'buy' affection by pleasing others. But it doesn't work, it undermines your confidence and can lower your self-esteem further.

You matter, baby!

If any of this strikes a chord, it can be painful to realise that your life is taking this pattern, but if you want it to change, you have to confront it. Where should you draw the line between being kind and being a doormat?

Your feelings could give you a clue, but most people who devote their lives to pleasing others have learned to blank out what they feel. Either they believe they are wrong to feel unhappy, or they believe that other people's feelings count more than

their own. To find out if this is true for you, why not ask yourself, 'Am I as important as other people?'

If your instinctive answer is 'No' (and you'd be amazed how common that is), ask yourself: 'Does this make me confident or happy?'

Think of a nursery with lots of babies asleep in their cribs. Would you go up to one of these innocents and put a label on its forehead saying, 'This child isn't as important as the others'? Of course you wouldn't. So why would you put such a label on your own head now that you're grown up? You're the one who's living your life. What you do affects you far more profoundly than it does anyone else. You matter!

Taking your feelings into account does not make you selfish. If you respect yourself and others equally, it's not selfish, it's being assertive, and it's good for your self-esteem. It's good for the people around you too because it means you value their capabilities and goodwill.

But once you realise that you are allowed to be assertive, the question is how? If you've been discounting your feelings, you may have found that when you do finally let them out you have built up such a head of steam that you can't help but yell! Or you may have become blameful and sarcastic, dishing out blanket criticisms. In either case, if you examine what you're really feeeling, you'll probably find it's anger.

Anger management

A lot of people might think that anger is always wrong or just plain nasty, but it isn't; it's there to protect you. The trick is to know that there's a big difference between feeling angry and losing your temper. Once you learn to recognise the signs that mean you're annoyed, you can do something about the problem before you blow up.

There's nothing wrong with saying something like, 'I'm feeling really stressed right now, so are you willing to give me a hand?' Then you can open negotiations. Clear communication lets you and the other person know where you both stand.

Saying, 'Will you vacuum the front room before tea tonight?' invites a response. It might be, 'Sure, no problem,' in which case the job gets done. Or it might be 'I can't do it tonight because I'll be late back, but I'll do it sometime tomorrow, OK?'

At this point one of two things can happen. Either the other person gets on with the job, or they don't. If you have been discounting your feelings you might then feel obliged to vacuum anyway, but that only gives the message that your requests don't need to be taken seriously.

What you could say is 'When you didn't vacuum the front room I was disappointed. Will you do it tonight please?' If the other person gets hostile that's their choice.

Be brave and change your life for the better

Being assertive may not work every time but it gives you the best chance of getting more of what you want. And knowing that you've acted on your feelings is good for your confidence.

Then there's saying no. As children we're taught not to say no to requests but there comes a point when it could be vital for your well-being. You don't have to be rude about it. It's perfectly acceptable to say something like, 'I'd love to help you but I'm really stretched so I'm afraid I can't.' The word 'no' doesn't even figure in there but you've made your position plain. Then you need to stick to your guns!

If you have spent a lifetime pleasing others at your own expense, it will take time, determination and courage to change, but the benefits will be enormous. Once you begin to value yourself and your feelings, your confidence will rise, your relationships will improve, and you'll have more energy for yourself. You might use some of it to relax and unwind. Or you might set yourself some small, achievable goals, such as making time for friends, to study, or to get to your Slimming World class every week.

Who knows? Those dreams that seemed so far out of reach could be just around the corner! □

This article first appeared in *Slimming World* Aug/Sept 2003

Task

Write an article on planning a family holiday with young children. It should be in a similar style to 'Reveal your super self!' and for the same audience. Try to include some of the issues below:

❋ where to go — expense, distance, time

❋ food — take your own, foreign foods, fussy eaters

❋ entertainment — expense, boredom, weather, arguments

❋ parents — need to relax, crèche, kids' club

❋ new experiences — good for children, can be exhausting

❋ delays — coping with stress, airports, railway stations

AO3(iii)

Use a range of sentence structures effectively with accurate punctuation and spelling

Key words	What the key words mean
use a range of sentence structures effectively	You should try to vary the length and types of sentences you use (see pages 91–92).
accurate punctuation	Full stops and commas should be used accurately. You need to know how and when to use inverted commas for speech or quotations. The exclamation mark and the question mark should be used appropriately. For Grade C and above you should be confident about using the colon, semi-colon and apostrophe.
accurate spelling	Spelling ability will range from 'some accuracy in the spelling of simple words' (Grade F/G) to 'a high level of accuracy in spelling' Grade (A/A*).

Aiming to learn accurate spelling, punctuation and grammar from a textbook alone is not realistic. Having said that, if you work through the following section you do stand a chance of improving in some areas that you find challenging.

Task

Rewrite the following passage, putting in the appropriate capital letters and punctuation.

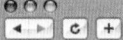

UK should 'reverse astronaut ban'

the uk should rethink its policy ban on astronauts a report written for the royal astronomical society (ras) says the report warns Britain risks being isolated on the international stage if it continues its longstanding refusal to fund the human exploration of space the ras expert panel says the cost of joining other nations with astronaut programmes could be some £150m a year but the scientific educational and economic benefits would be worth it panel member professor ken pounds of the university of leicester said it is hard to imagine that the uk one of the worlds leading economies would not be fully involved in a global scientific and technology endeavour with such strong potential to inspire we therefore recommend that the government re-evaluates its long-standing opposition to british involvement in human space exploration

The exercise above is intended to get you thinking and it is not something you have to do in an exam. It is a reminder though that, without clear punctuation, writing is difficult to read and understand. In your exam you need to make sure that what you are saying is as clear as possible to the examiner. If he/she has to do a lot of the work for you, as you did in the exercise, then you are not going to get high marks. Punctuating your work is good manners — it helps to get you marks, and not just those that are specifically allocated for spelling and punctuation.

The two punctuation marks most likely to prevent you gaining high marks are the full stop and the apostrophe.

Full stops

First, let's look at some student writing:

> We stayed in the hotel in Magic Kingdom it was amazing even if you don't like Mickey Mouse now I can guarantee that by the time you come home you will love him.

The problem with this student's work is a common one. The writing is in sentences and has some variety of sentence structure, but full stops have been forgotten. Your thoughts may run on, but you need to put a full stop every time you complete a unit of meaning.

This is an improved version of the passage above. Look carefully at where the full stops are:

> We stayed in the hotel in Magic Kingdom. It was amazing. Even if you don't like Mickey Mouse now, I can guarantee that by the time you come home you will love him.

The content is the same but the writing is now clearer and would gain more credit. Note also the addition of the comma. Commas are sometimes confused with full stops as they are both a kind of pause. Look again at the example above. If a full stop had been used — 'Even if you don't like Mickey mouse now.' — it would have been wrong, as that part of the sentence is not a complete unit of meaning.

Here is another student example:

> I went to America last summer, as a holiday I would recommend it, there is so much to do and so many places to see.

This student has written in sentences, but has put commas at the end of them instead of full stops. You may have heard that 'a sentence is a complete thought'. This is true, but a complete thought can be made up of several sentences. If you read the above text again you can see that each of the three sections divided by commas is a complete unit of meaning.

If the student had written, 'When I look back on my trip, **I remember how friendly people were**, even in New York', commas would have been used

correctly. The only part of this sentence which is a complete unit of meaning is the part in bold. You could not just write, 'When I look back on my trip' or 'even in New York'.

If you find that you have written several lines without a full stop, go back and check — you have probably missed some full stops. Getting your full stops in the right places will improve your grade.

Apostrophes

Look back at the passage entitled 'UK should "reverse astronaut ban"' on page 88. Did you use an apostrophe in 'world's'? And did you wonder if you needed an apostrophe in the three instances of 'its'? (You didn't.)

Lots of people, not just GCSE students, have problems using the apostrophe correctly because it has two functions:

* to show that a letter or letters have been missed out
* to indicate a possessive

You probably feel confident with the first use, but try the task to test yourself.

> ### Task
> Write out the following and put the apostrophe in exactly the right place:
> I wouldnt do that if theres any danger of frost as it isnt likely to survive low temperatures. Id hate you to lose it. Havent you got anywhere better to keep it?

The second use needs a bit of care, but you need to get it right if you want to achieve a good grade. There are four basic rules:

* If the word is singular, add *'s*, e.g. Simon's jumper, yesterday's paper.
* If the word is plural and does not end in *s*, add *'s*, e.g. women's skirts, people's opinions.
* If the word is plural and ends in *s* then add *'* only, e.g. the boys' school, the Smiths' house.
* Never use an apostrophe with possessive pronouns, i.e. its, ours, yours, theirs, hers. You need to take special care with 'its', e.g. the dog lost its tail.

Don't get obsessed with using apostrophes — they do not occur all that often. Examiners don't want to see writing like this:

> When it start's to rain, all the chair's get soaked and everyone rushe's around to get umbrella's and raincoat's.

Finally, a reminder about inverted commas (sometimes called speech marks or quotation marks; you should have used some in the 'UK should "reverse astronaut ban"' task): they only go round the actual words spoken. See how well you do in the following task. (You will also need to apply what you have just read about apostrophes.)

4

Task

Put the inverted commas, apostrophes and any capital letters needed in the correct places in the following sentences:

1 I think thats all I can do today said the plumber. Ill come back tomorrow when its dry and finish the job.

2 My mother always tells my father you never listen to anything I say. Shes right.

3 Youve only got 10 minutes he warned but you might make it to the doctors surgery before it closes.

4 Dont do that he shouted its too heavy to lift.

Using a range of sentences

Read the following piece of student writing. Think about what impression you get of the writer's ability from the sentence structure:

> We climbed the gate. We switched on our torches. We were walking for about 10 minutes. Suddenly we heard someone scream. We rushed over to where we heard the screaming. There was no one there. Then we saw something white. We first thought it was a ghost. Then we saw it was a piece of clothing.

Do you agree that the writer's use of so many simple sentences makes it sound a bit childish? With a little more thought, the writer could have made the narrative flow more smoothly. Here is the same piece, but with some variation in the sentence structure:

> Having climbed over the gate, we switched on our torches. We had walked for about 10 minutes when suddenly we heard a scream. We rushed over to where we heard the screaming but there was no one there. We saw something white. We first thought it was a ghost but later realised it was a piece of clothing.

Several of the sentences, though still in the same order, have been joined together using various simple conjunctions. Note that one short sentence has been left as this creates an impact. The occasional short sentence can be effective.

Task

Look back at any piece of writing you have done and check your own work.

Look at the sets of commonly used conjunctions. They will be familiar to you, but do you use them in your writing?

Conjunctions that link meanings	Conjunctions that suggest opposite meanings
after	although
also	but
and	either...or
as	neither...nor
because	except
if	than
since	though
so	unless
that	whereas
until	yet
when	
wherever	
while	

Note: 'then' always starts a new sentence or clause — it is not a conjunction.

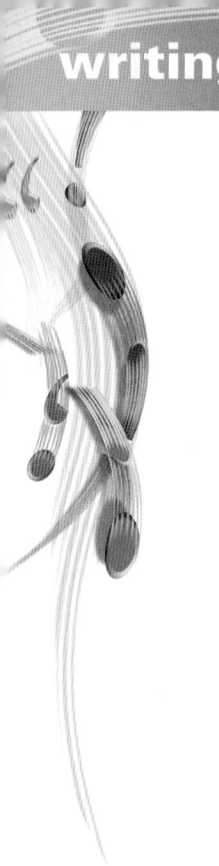

Another useful group is **linking words**, which usually come at the start of a sentence. They help to connect one sentence to another and can be used to link clauses, especially if they are surrounded by commas. Examples of these words are:

| however | nevertheless | notwithstanding | on the other hand | therefore |

Task

For each of the following groups of simple sentences think of **two** ways of combining them into one sentence. You can change the order of the sentences if you wish but do not change the meaning.

1 London is the capital of the UK. It is an interesting and exciting place to visit. It has lots of shops and theatres. It has many museums.

2 I looked at my watch. It was 5 o'clock in the morning. It was too early to get up. I couldn't get back to sleep.

3 We finally arrived at the airport. It was crowded. It was hot. We had nowhere to sit. My little sister started crying.

Sentence structure checklist

Whenever you write, get into the habit of leaving yourself time to do a 'health check' on your sentence structure. Questions to ask yourself are:

✳ How many times have I used 'and'? The examiner does not want to read '…and we did this and we went there and we saw…'.

✳ Have I started several sentences in the same way, for example using 'I', 'It is', 'Then' or 'Next'?

✳ Have I used some linking words? The examiner will give you credit for 'joined-up thinking'.

✳ Are all my sentences roughly the same length? Remember that the occasional short sentence can be effective.

Spelling

Some people find spelling more difficult than others. If you have a problem with spelling, here are a few tips to help you improve:

✳ Look back over your writing. Are there words that you keep misspelling? If so, make a list and **learn** the correct spelling. (There is no easy way round this.)

✳ If you really have a blind spot over a word (and most of us do have a few words that we find difficult to spell), try substituting another word. The list below gives some examples:

Word	Substitute	Word	Substitute
exaggerate	overstate	argument	dispute
occurred	happened	seize	grab/grasp
accommodate	find room for	disappear	vanish
necessary	needed	surprising	unexpected
beginning	start	choose	select
believe	trust/think	nuisance	problem/trouble

The English spelling system is not always logical or easy. Beware of words that sound the same but are spelled differently depending on their meaning. Make sure you know the difference. For example:

there, their, they're	to, two, too	whose, who's	your, you're

The examinations

English
Paper 1 Section A

Reading response to unseen non-fiction and media texts

Paper 1 Section A of the English GCSE examination is the only point at which you are faced with unseen material. It differs from other sections of the examination, which require you to answer a single, broad question that covers a number of Assessment Objectives (AOs) at the same time. In Paper 1 Section A, the Assessment Objectives are tested through a number of smaller, targeted questions.

The key to success is understanding what the questions set out to achieve and how they should be tackled. This chapter demonstrates how to analyse the paper and approach each question in turn. It also shows how the examiners would evaluate some sample responses.

The individual Assessment Objectives for reading are covered in Section 1 of this book, but it is useful to be reminded of them while considering this part of the examination.

AO2(i)	Read with insight and engagement, making appropriate references to texts and developing and sustaining interpretations of them.
AO2(ii)	Distinguish between fact and opinion and evaluate how information is presented.
AO2(iii)	Follow an argument, identifying implications and recognising inconsistencies.
AO2(iv)	Select material appropriate to your purpose, collate material from different sources, and make cross-references.
AO2(v)	Understand and evaluate how writers use linguistic, structural and presentational devices to achieve their effects, and comment on ways language varies and changes.

Answering the questions in Section A can be seen as a two-stage process:
1 Preparation and analysis
2 Execution (writing the answer)

Careful preparation is vital. You will see from the sample paper on page 97 that Section A has, in effect, five questions and if you are to allow yourself enough time to tackle Section B, you have 1 hour at the most to complete

them. It is easy under timed conditions to become muddled or to lose sight of exactly what you are supposed to be doing. However, if you have prepared the ground properly, your answers will be precise and you should avoid the risk of wandering off the subject.

> **Remember:** time spent in proper preparation is time saved in actually writing your answers.

Preparation

Your first task is to identify where each of the Assessment Objectives is tested. If you know what the question is testing, you will be able to answer it more effectively.

1 Read through the questions in the sample paper below and identify what each question is asking you to do.
2 Look at the total marks for each question. You should double the mark and spend roughly that number of minutes on the question (e.g. 4 marks × 2 = 8 minutes).
3 Make sure that you know what is coming next so you don't use the same material in two answers.

Sample paper: Section A

Answer all questions in this section.

1 Read **Item 1**, the foreword to the book *Extreme Ironing* by Phil Shaw.
  a What arguments does Phil Shaw put forward to promote extreme ironing as a sport?   *(4 marks)*
  b How does the writer use facts and opinions to support his argument?   *(4 marks)*

Now read **Item 2**, the Tefal advertisement for a steam iron.
  c **Compare** the views about ironing in **Item 2**, the advertisement for the Tefal iron, and **Item 1**, the foreword to *Extreme Ironing*. You should only answer this question by referring to the text in each item.   *(6 marks)*

2 a How do the pictures in the two **Items** show different attitudes towards men and women?   *(7 marks)*
  b How effective are the presentational and organisational devices in **Item 2**?   *(6 marks)*

Analysis of the questions

1 What do the questions test?

✳ Question 1a is a 'follow an argument' question, or 'what is Phil Shaw trying to say?' (AO2(iii)).

✳ Question 1b is asking about 'fact and opinion' (AO2(ii)).

✳ Question 1c is a 'compare' question, which is made obvious by the word 'compare' being in bold (AO2(iv)). It is also in part a 'follow an argument' question (AO2(iii)).

✳ Questions 2a and 2b are media questions, so you have to reread the two items as media texts.

✳ Question 2a covers just about all of the Assessment Objectives, but remember that you must use some media terms and media ideas or concepts.

> **Remember:** most questions require you to use the 'PEE' formula (see page 29), so therefore cover Assessment Objective 2(i).

✳ Question 2b asks about presentational and organisational devices (AO2(v)).

2 Check the mark totals

✳ You will see how important the mark totals are when you come to the mark scheme. As Section A has a number of short questions it is important that you spend the appropriate amount of time on each.

✳ Note that the marks for each question part are fairly equal, so you must not miss out a question or you could slip down a whole grade — 4–5 marks equals about a grade in this part of the examination.

3 Check the instructions

✳ After reading through the whole paper and identifying any possible places where the same material could be used, you can read Item 1.

✳ Note that you are asked to read Item 1 before reading Item 2. It is always best to do what the paper tells you.

Task

Read Item 1 (opposite) and then answer question 1a on p. 97.

Item 1: Extreme ironing

There is a small group of people who will travel to the very ends of the Earth in search of new challenges. They will risk everything for the experience of adventure and danger. For them, nature itself is not enough of a challenge. These people are extreme ironists. Extreme ironing is the latest adenaline sport — combining the thrills of outdoor activity with the satisfaction of a well-pressed shirt.

Most ironists love the thrill of combining the everyday with the exiting. Ask a mountaineer why he or she climbs, they often answer, 'Because it's there.' An extreme ironist irons his or her clothes, 'Because they're creased.'

Over the years I tried my hand at a number of so-called extreme sports. Rock climbing, scuba diving, surfing, abseiling, caving and mountain biking — I tried them all. But in each case I was left wanting that little bit extra. I found what I was looking for in extreme ironing.

It is fair to say that the sport is now a global phenomenon with sports men and women from some 20 countries taking ironing to the edge and beyond. The sport has come on a long way since its birth in the city of Leicester, England, in 1997. There are now regular events, competitions and a number of websites dedicated to the sport. September 2002 saw the first World Championships with 80 competitors from 10 countries going iron-to-iron in extreme outdoor conditions.

This book has been written as a complete guide to everything you'll ever need to know about the world's first white goods extreme sport. For newcomers, the basics of extreme ironing are explained with attention paid to all aspects, from choosing your iron to selecting your fabric. Later on, the different styles of extreme ironing are described and, in the final section of the book, competitive extreme ironing is explored.

Extreme ironing has given me a great deal of satisfaction over the years. To me, there's no other sport that matches it for excitement, danger or skill. Next time you are ironing your shirt for work on a Sunday evening, just think, you could have taken it outside and joined the latest sporting craze: extreme ironing.

Foreword to *Extreme Ironing* by Phil Shaw, New Holland 2003.

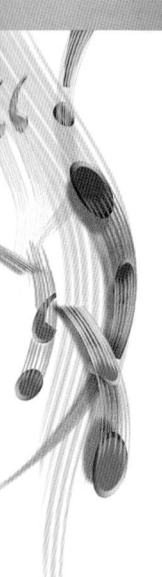

Task

When you have completed your answer to question 1a, turn to the sample responses at the end of this section (pages 103–107) and ask yourself:

❋ Which band of marks would I put the student's response in? Use the ladder of skills below to help you decide.

❋ What skills are being shown?

❋ How does my answer compare with this one?

Band	Skills descriptors
'detailed/shaped and absorbed' 4 marks Grade A/A*	❋ clear and detailed understanding of the question ❋ material fully absorbed and shaped for purpose ❋ response is as detailed as you could expect from a 16-year-old
'clear attempt' 3 marks Grade C/B	❋ clear attempt to engage with the task ❋ structured response that selects and comments on different aspects of the question ❋ some of the language of the original retained
'attempt' 2 marks Grade E/D	❋ candidate attempts to answer the question ❋ main impression is that the order and language of item 1 has been retained ❋ candidate tends to identify ❋ candidate tends to paraphrase
'little evidence' 1 mark Grade G/F	❋ little evidence that the candidate understands the task ❋ mainly paraphrased or copied ❋ general/descriptive comment ❋ little content

Task

Answer question 1b in the sample paper on p. 97, taking into account the following points:

❋ It has a total of 4 marks.

❋ It is asking you to show **how** the writer uses facts and opinions to support his argument.

❋ Which band of marks will you end up in if you simply identify (or 'spot') facts and opinions?

❋ Do not try to find all of the facts and opinions: try to work out the general use that the writer is making of facts and opinions throughout the whole passage.

❋ You will get a Grade C or higher if you explain the use of at least one fact and one opinion.

Task

Use the ladder of skills on page 100 and the sample answers on pages 103–107 to mark another student's answer.

Item 2: Tefal steam iron advertisement

Task

Now read Item 2, the Tefal steam iron advertisement, and look at question 1c on p. 97.

1 Copy the following chart and fill in the two boxes on views about ironing in Items 1 and 2.

Views about ironing in Item 1	Comparison words	Views about ironing in Item 2

What you have just done is to identify and list the differences and similarities between the two, or to **juxtapose** them. In the question you are actually being asked to compare the two items, so you must use a variety of comparing words. Note that AO(iii) asks you to 'identify implications and recognise inconsistencies' — in other words, to find the ways in which the two items are the same and different.

2 Now write in a comparison word for each of the points in your lists. For example:

Views about ironing in Item 1	Comparison words	Views about ironing in Item 2
it is an exciting and exhilarating sport	however	it is a dreary and time-consuming chore that makes you mad
ironing can be made more interesting by taking up the sport of extreme ironing	similarly	ironing can be made more effortless by buying a Tefal steam iron

3 Now convert your notes in the chart into sentences, writing the comparison word(s) in a different colour. If you can do this, it shows you have made a 'clear attempt at a comparison' and should at least qualify for the C-grade band of marks.

Task

Now answer question 2a on p. 97. It is constructed in a similar way to question 1c, but instead of comparing views you are asked to compare the pictures. You must also think about what the pictures suggest about attitudes towards men and women.

Now read question 2b and write your own answer. Note that it is only referring to Item 2, the advertisement. You are asked to keep several variables in your head while answering it:
❋ How are presentational and organisational devices used?
❋ How well do they work?

Try to write a sentence or two about three of the following:
❋ the picture
❋ the font used by the copywriter
❋ the way the advertisement is laid out on the page
❋ the inset picture and text
❋ the headings

Task

When you have completed all the questions on the sample paper, read the responses below and review your work in the light of the examiner's comments.

The more you understand about how this paper is constructed and marked, the better you will perform in the examination.

Sample answers and examiner's comments

Question 1a

What arguments does Phil Shaw put forward to promote extreme ironing as a sport?

Student answer 1

There is a small group of people who will travel the Earth in search of new challenges. They have already tried their hand at a number of so-called extreme sports like rock climbing, there's no other sport that matches it for excitement.

Examiner's comment

The candidate has identified pieces of information in the passage and copied them out. Though there is evidence that he has read the text, there is **little evidence** of understanding.

This is a response in the lowest band of marks because it does not offer any comment and is mainly copying or simple selection. It would receive Grade F/G.

> **Do not** simply copy out pieces of text.

Student answer 2

Phil Shaw mainly argues that extreme ironing is the latest adrenaline sport and that it combines mountaineering and an everyday pastime like ironing. This sport gives that little bit extra to those people who have tried everything and it is worth doing 'Because they're creased.' It is now a worldwide sport, which began in Leicester and is now carried on in 10 countries across the world.

Examiner's comment

This answer is close to the original words but the candidate **attempts** to answer the question. For example, she points out that 'Phil Shaw mainly argues that…'. However, the quotation that the candidate has chosen, 'Because they're creased', is not actually an argument put forward to promote extreme ironing as a sport. This shows that she has no real understanding of the question.

She will probably **identify** features in some of the ensuing questions on this paper. This type of candidate often only reads the beginning, or first half, of a text, thus limiting the detail and level of understanding of the response. Such candidates tend to read one paragraph at a time and to **paraphrase** each of these paragraphs. This takes a long time, so they tend not to write as much as they should. (Length is not something you are assessed on, however; you will see this when you look at the best response to this question.) This candidate would receive Grade D/E.

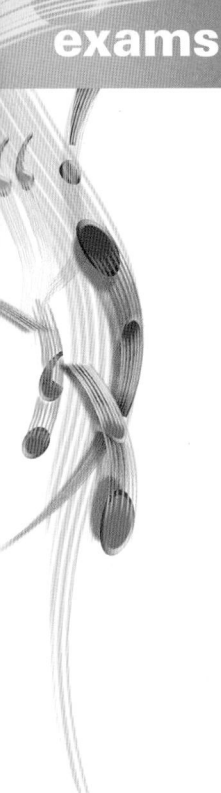

Student answer 3

Phil Shaw puts forward several arguments for people to take up extreme ironing, the main one being that it is the latest adrenaline sport. It also builds on and adds more to other extreme sports like rock climbing and scuba diving. He argues that it is a global phenomenon with many regular events and a website and a World Championships first held in 2002. He finally argues that it adds excitement and satisfaction to what can be a boring and unexciting task.

Examiner's comment

This is better than the second candidate's effort because it is a **clear attempt** to answer the question. The candidate puts the arguments **in an order** and **understands** that there is a main argument. The answer goes beyond simply listing information and ranges over the whole text. Some words and phrases are recognisable from the original text, but the student does more than paraphrase.

It is not, however, a fully organised response. The candidate tends to jump from one point to the next without there being a clear connection between points. He would gain a Grade C.

Student answer 4

The author, Phil Shaw, puts forward several arguments for the promotion of the sport of extreme ironing. First, he argues that it combines the best of more accepted extreme sports with the everyday task of ironing. He promotes it by arguing that he has tried the rest and this is the best. He also promotes it by legitimising it because it has its own World Championships and a website. His final argument is that extreme ironing will give you a lot of satisfaction if you follow the advice given in the rest of the book.

Examiner's comment

Here is a list of reasons why this answer is so good:

❖ The candidate has fully **absorbed** the whole passage and has **shaped** the material to answer the question.
❖ The candidate clearly itemises the main arguments for extreme ironing — 'first', 'also' and 'final' — and presents them in a logical sequence.
❖ This candidate has used few words from the passage, and the reader never gets the sense that the answer is simply paraphrase.
❖ The candidate is in touch with the passage — there are continuous and detailed references to it.

Notice how the answer starts with the phrase 'The author', which tells the examiner that this candidate understands there is a writer behind the text who has an argument he wishes to put across to the reader. This answer would receive a Grade A.

Question 1b

How does the writer use facts and opinions to support his argument?

Student answer 1

One fact that Phil Shaw uses is that there was a World Championship in 2002. He uses this fact to show the reader that extreme ironing is a legitimate sport, which has its own championships.

  One of the opinions he uses is that extreme ironing is the latest adrenaline sport. This is the writer's opinion because many more adrenaline sports may have been created since he wrote this and it is only his opinion that extreme ironing leads to a rush of adrenaline.

Examiner's comment

This student has clearly identified one fact and one opinion and has attempted to explain the use made of these by the writer. She would achieve a Grade C.

Student answer 2

The author of this passage tends to use facts to legitimise this new sport of extreme ironing by giving a mixture of dates, places and facts about its world-wide acceptance and popularity. He also uses facts to prove that this rather unlikely sport actually exists! He tends to use opinions to bolster his argument that this is the best and most exciting of sports. He tends to use unsubstantiated personal views in an exaggerated manner (e.g. 'To me, there's no other sport that matches it for excitement').

Examiner's comment

This is a good example of a student who has fully **absorbed** the passage and **shapes** the general reasons why the writer uses both facts and opinions. Unlike some weaker students, this candidate does not quote at length. There is a brief supporting quotation at the end, but the overall response shows that the candidate understands the reasons behind the writer's use of facts and opinions. He recognises that a writer might use facts and opinions for more than one reason and comes up with interesting and valid reasons why. The answer would gain a Grade A.

Question 2

a *How do the pictures in the two Items show different attitudes towards men and women?*

b *How effective are the presentational and organisational devices in Item 2?*

Student answer 1

The pictures in the first item show that ironing can be an exciting and exhilarating sport for men. However, the second item shows that it is a dreary and time-consuming

task carried out by good-looking young women, because it shows a woman blowing off steam at the thought of ironing. This is the opposite of what an extreme ironist thinks of ironing.

Examiner's comment

This is a clear comparison between the use made of pictures in the two items on ironing. It is not detailed, however, and an examiner would not award the candidate a mark in the C/B band without more explanation, or some direct use of media terms.

Student answer 2

There is a very different, but equally sexist, view of ironing presented in the two items because of their different purposes and audiences. The first item puts across the rather odd view that ironing is an exciting and thoroughly modern sport in the twenty-first century aimed at men. The view conveyed in the pictures is one of men ironing in extreme conditions, i.e. on precarious mountain tops.

The second item is also on the subject of ironing and this advertisement does try to stress that if you use this iron, then you will enjoy the experience of ironing more because it will be easier and safer. On the other hand, the foreword suggests that although ironing can be satisfying, it can only really be a white-knuckle sport for men. This is a very different view of ironing and one that is contrasted by the picture of a pretty young woman who is obviously mad at the thought of conventional steam ironing. This view would appeal to the target audience of middle-aged housewives who are not, maybe, as good-looking as the model in the advert.

Examiner's comment

This answer is not only longer, but it is more focused than the first answer and looks at media concepts such as purpose, audience and the specific use of language aimed at persuading two different readerships.

In the C/B band the mark scheme states 'some appropriate media terminology', but in the A/A* band it states 'sophisticated and convincing use of technical terminology to describe media concepts'. What this means is that to gain an A/A* you need to do more than simply use media terminology: you must have some idea of how a media text works.

This candidate not only uses media terminology (e.g. 'purpose and audience'), but also demonstrates an understanding that the texts are in different media (an article and an advertisement) and that both use the accepted conventions of their respective medium. On the other hand, the answer lacks a detailed consideration of the pictures themselves. This would have been needed to make a sophisticated media point, so the candidate would thus gain 6 rather than 7 marks and a grade in the A/A* band.

Student answer 3

There is a black and white picture of a woman blowing off steam. There is also a close-up picture of some irons at the bottom of the page to show what you get for your money. There is also a sort of headline and sub-heading with quite short paragraphs.

Examiner's comment

This response does no more than identify presentational and organisational devices. There is no attempt to comment on what the pictures suggest. If the student had evaluated how effective the devices had been, he would have moved up at least one grade from the awarded E/F. The response would be improved by including phrases such as:

- This presentational device works well because...
- This is less successful, in my opinion, because...
- Both of these linked devices are used to...

The response would then read:

> *There is a black and white picture of a woman blowing off steam at the thought of normal ironing. This presentational device works well because it initially draws the reader's attention. There is also a close-up picture of some irons at the bottom of the page to show what you get for your money. This is less successful, in my opinion, because it is only a minor detail and it detracts from the overall effect of the advertisement. There is also a sort of headline and sub-heading with quite a short paragraph. Both of these linked devices are used, like the photograph, to draw the reader's attention. However, I think that they have another, deeper purpose from the advertiser's point of view. They make the advertisement look like a newspaper story and help to give more truth to the message that the advertisers are trying to put across.*

This is a perfectly clear response to the question because it:

- is written in some detail
- evaluates each of the points made
- shows understanding of how the devices can affect the reader's response
- makes some careful use of examples to back up the answer
- shows that the student has thought about and organised the material fully

The answer fulfils most of the points as set out in the mark scheme, so the examiner would put it in the highest band. This is a clear and detailed response and is as much as one can expect a candidate to produce in about 12 minutes for 5–6 marks. There may be better answers, but remember, the examiners are not expecting perfection.

English
Paper 1 Section B
Writing to argue, persuade or advise

Writing to argue and persuade

These two forms of writing are easily confused because they are similar in many ways. Essentially, an **argument** aims to **prove** a point in an organised and reasoned way, whereas **persuasive writing** aims to **influence** the reader in a certain way.

For example, medical scientists have **argued** the dangers of smoking. Their purpose was to present the evidence of their research so as to demonstrate the risks and consequences of smoking. Anti-smoking campaigners, on the other hand, have used this evidence to **persuade** people to want to give up smoking. In other words, argument **presents** ideas and persuasion **uses** ideas in order to influence people.

Let's take a fun example that isn't too muddled up with real-life issues. First, here is an argument in favour of yellow cars:

All cars should be painted yellow because there would be huge savings in the costs of providing a range of finishes. Time would be saved in ordering cars of a particular colour and touch-up paint would always be available. Customers would save time deciding which colour car to buy.

There would be a probable reduction in accidents, as yellow is more visible than most other colours.

Second, here is persuasive writing on the same subject:

Wouldn't it make life simpler if all cars were painted yellow? Just think, there would be no more agonising over what colour your next car should be and there would be no more frustrating wait while your special finish was on order. What's more, if you were unlucky enough to damage your car, the paint for a touch-up or respray would always be available.

You would also find your car would be cheaper because manufacturers wouldn't have to stock vast ranges of fancy paints, and an added bonus is that you would be more visible and safer in cheerful bright yellow than in gloomy grey or black.

Both passages use the same information but there are important differences. The argument piece consists of an impersonal set of reasons why cars should all be painted yellow. The most important feature of an argument is that **statements must be justified with reasons**. It is then up to the reader to agree or disagree. The persuasion piece is directed at the readers personally and tries to convince them that they should *want* yellow cars. It also gives reasons for the claim that cars should be painted yellow, but instead of being impersonal, the reasons, although similar to those given in the argument, are all linked to the reader's wellbeing and enjoyment.

Note that the second passage is a little longer — not because it contains any more information, but because of the way its ideas are presented. The passage uses a number of persuasive devices:

1 It opens with a question directed at the reader that should have only one answer: 'yes.'
2 There are a number of loaded phrases that reinforce the idea of making life easier for the reader: 'no more agonising', 'no more frustrating wait', 'always be available', 'added bonus', 'more visible and safer'.
3 It uses repetition to emphasise the point: 'no more agonising', 'no more frustrating wait'.
4 It uses adjectives to manipulate the reader's point of view. The normal range of finishes is described as 'fancy', but the yellow is 'cheerful' and 'bright' and contrasts with 'gloomy' grey or black.

Language such as this, which is designed to influence the reader as well as to present information, is called **rhetorical** language.

Task

1 Present the **arguments** in favour of designing all televisions sets so that they work for only 4 hours per day.

2 Write a short piece **persuading** people to buy televisions that work for only 4 hours per day.

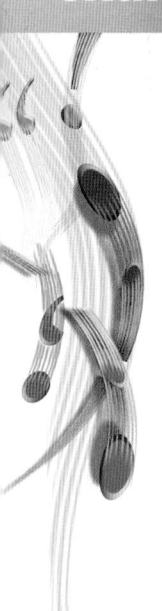

Argument

Considering other points of view

Look again at the argument for painting cars yellow. Although all the points are firmly backed up with reasons, they represent only one point of view. The argument ignores any opposing opinions.

Arguments can be strengthened if they **anticipate** a different point of view. You may feel strongly about an issue, with excellent reasons, but it is always a good idea to imagine what someone who disagrees with you might say and to build a defence into your argument.

For example, many people reading about the advantages of painting cars yellow would simply dismiss the idea, saying 'It would be so boring', and that would be the end of your case. What do you do about it? Try to head them off. You could write something on these lines:

> No doubt some would argue that painting all cars yellow would simply be too boring. Of course, none of us wants to be bored, but that is purely an emotional response. The real question is whether people's fancies about a little bit of extra colour are more important than the real savings in the cost of motoring.

Notice how there's an imaginary duel occuring now, like the cut and thrust of a fencing match:

1 First you allow an opposing opinion: 'too boring'.

2 Then you even appear to agree with it: 'Of course,…'.

3 But at the same time you counterattack by devaluing the objection, saying it is 'purely an emotional response', which suggests it is not a considered thought.

4 Finally, you ram home your advantage by setting 'real savings' against 'people's fancies'.

In this case the use of words and phrases such as 'of course', 'purely emotional' and 'fancies' is rhetorical, or loaded for effect. This shows how, when you are trying to prove a point, argument actually borders on persuasion.

> **Task**
>
> Look again at what you have written in support of limiting television viewing to 4 hours a day. Rewrite the piece to take account of the most obvious objections.

Gathering your thoughts and ideas

Real-life issues tend to be less clear cut than the question of whether we should paint cars yellow. Before you can start writing your argument you must gather your ideas. These should include:

* what **facts** you know about the subject
* your **personal opinions**
* the ideas of those who take a **different view** from yourself

In many ways this preparation is the most important part of the process of writing a successful argument.

It is important not to confuse expressing your personal feelings with presenting an argument. For example, it is not enough to say 'I think experimenting on animals is wrong', even if the thought makes you cry. To turn that opinion into an argument, you must have facts and reasons. Your argument can be passionate but it must be more than a list of unsupported personal opinions.

The same process of gathering your thoughts and ideas applies whether you are preparing to write an argument or preparing to persuade. The obvious way to do this is to make a list. For example, if you had to write about whether it is right that smoking should be banned in all public places, you might construct a list on these lines:

1 Smoking kills
2 1,600 people die per week in the UK — 5 million worldwide
3 Bar staff need protecting
4 People should be free to choose
5 Non-smokers have no choice
6 Nanny state
7 Personal choice
8 Passive smoking
9 People enjoy smoking
10 Loss of trade
11 Encouragement better than compulsion
12 Smoking relaxes
13 We ban drugs etc.
14 Alcohol as dangerous as tobacco
15 Number of deaths beginning to fall

There is more than enough material here. Be careful that you don't fall into the trap of dealing with the ideas in the order in which you listed them. To turn points like these into an argument, you must present them in a sensible order so that your ideas flow and develop naturally.

Example of student performance

Student answer

I don't think smoking should be allowed because it kills about 1,600 people a week. We should protect bar staff who are exposed to smoke all the time. People should be free to choose but non-smokers have no choice.

Some people say we live in a nanny state and I think personal choice is important. People enjoy smoking a lot. I know lots of my friends are always smoking and

try to get me to join them. But I say, why should you smoke and drink because they both can kill?

I've heard that lots of people are giving up smoking and the number of deaths is dropping. That shows it would be a good idea to ban it now.

Examiner's comment

The candidate's work has a number of good points, with a useful statistic, and the basic ideas are communicated clearly. The vocabulary is appropriate.

However, the sequence of ideas is not clear and the personal anecdote ('lots of my friends…') only loosely connects with the points that surround it. Apart from one use of the word 'but' there are no words to link the ideas, which are presented largely as a list of separate items. Moreover, there is an apparent contradiction between the statement that smoking should not be allowed and that people should be free to choose.

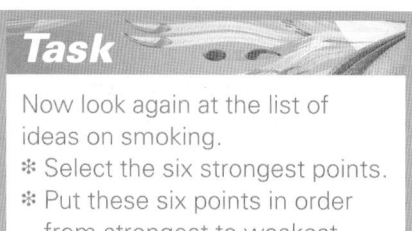

Task

Now look again at the list of ideas on smoking.
* Select the six strongest points.
* Put these six points in order from strongest to weakest.

It is a good idea to jot down your points in a more flexible way that allows you to think about how they connect. There is no single way of doing this; a lot depends on how familiar the subject is. If it is a matter close to your heart, you may have some well-developed ideas on the subject and you won't require much of a written plan. But even then you must make sure that you are really dealing with the question that is asked, not a similar one you have practised and know a lot about. For example, the question 'Should the laws on drug use be changed?' is not the same as 'How can the use of drugs by young people be reduced?' Much of the material would be the same, but it would be used in a different way. It is always a good idea to remind yourself of your exact subject to give yourself a clear focus.

Many students find it useful to lay out their ideas in an open plan that might look something like Plan 1 (opposite). Putting the subject at the centre of the notes helps keep it in mind. Even students who have plenty to say frequently lose marks because they drift off the subject.

The next stage in the process is to wire up your ideas to create some joined-up thinking. People often refer to lines of thought, so let's draw some lines. First you must decide where to start. It's always a good idea to begin with a bang. Make a positive point to launch your argument. Then find the facts and ideas that link with your starting point. Your joined-up plan might look like Plan 2. Note that not every point is used.

Plan 1

Plan 2

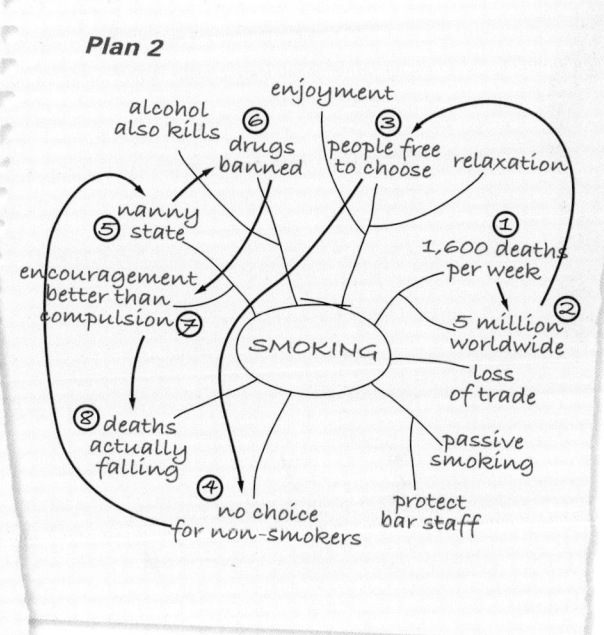

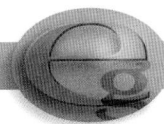

Example of student performance

Student answer based on Plan 2

A ban on smoking in public places would save many lives. Smoking kills about 1,600 people a week in the UK and about 5 million worldwide. Some might say that it is solely a matter of freedom of choice, but what choice have the millions of passive smokers who are forced to breathe in noxious fumes created by others exercising their freedom?

On the other hand, it is said that we live in a nanny state and there is too much control over our lives. However, it is the government's responsibility to protect all citizens and laws are necessary. For example, we do not allow the free use of drugs and we have many laws, such as the compulsory wearing of seatbelts and food hygiene regulations, which we all accept.

Nevertheless, it is always better if there is public support for new laws and there is some evidence that fewer people are smoking already, so a ban would be widely welcomed.

The highlighted words can be referred to as **signal words**. They steer the argument by signalling changes of direction. These words are vital when you are handling different points of view. You can use them to add ideas and to switch from one point of view to another. You can also use sentences on these lines: 'Although some people argue X, Y is…'; 'Despite the fact that some people say X, Y is…'

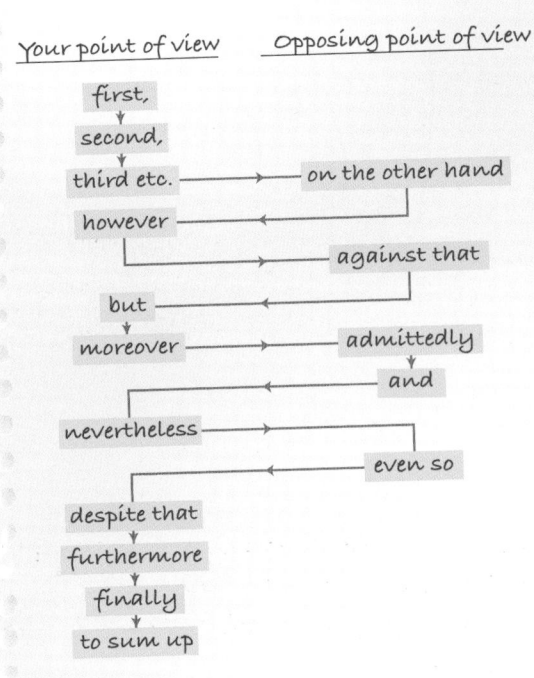

The diagram on the left shows how an argument can be organised to take account of and answer views opposing your own. It is always a good idea to begin with some firm points, so you might open with clear statements setting out your ideas, as indicated on the left-hand side of the diagram (first, second, third etc.). Then, using the words 'on the other hand', you introduce one of the objections to your point of view. Obviously, you do not agree with the opposing point, so you use 'however' to lead the argument back to an even stronger point of your own, which answers the objection. It is advisable not to use the same signal word too many times, so the next time you introduce an opposing point of view you could use 'against that' rather than repeat 'however'.

You probably do not use words such as 'moreover' in everyday conversation, so it is important that you learn to use them properly. It is not enough simply to drop them into your writing regardless of the wider sense.

Task

Below is a list of points on the subject of whether there should be a ban on school students wearing special dress associated with their religion.

✳ Individual freedom
✳ School uniform should be for all
✳ Human rights

Task (continued)

* Religious duty
* School rules necessary — need for order
* Religious tradition
* French ban on religious dress in schools
* Special treatment
* What about wearing Christian crosses?
* Respect for people's beliefs
* Islamic jilbab
* Sikh turban allowed
* Why shouldn't all students wear what they want?

1 Set the items out in the form of a diagram.

2 Decide whether you agree or disagree.

3 Connect the points so as to support your point of view.

Task

Write an **argument** that doctors should be spending their time curing people rather than carrying out cosmetic surgery.

Persuasion

For the purposes of the examination, the main preparation work for a piece of persuasive writing is exactly the same as that for an argument. You need to gather facts and ideas and organise them into a sensible order, in the same way shown for arguments on pages 110–114.

Once you have done that, however, you need to think a little differently about how to present your thoughts and there are some special techniques you need to consider.

Tone and audience

Generally speaking, argument uses cool and detached language and tries as far as possible to be impersonal, even when putting forward a powerful point of view. Often the writer is 'invisible' and the use of the word 'I' is avoided. The scientific argument for the existence of global warming is a good example. If the scientists who claim that the climate is being severely affected by human activity were too emotional, their arguments would be seen as biased and would therefore carry less weight.

Persuasive writing, on the other hand, deliberately sets out to influence the reader by appealing to the emotions, so it is important that the writing conveys

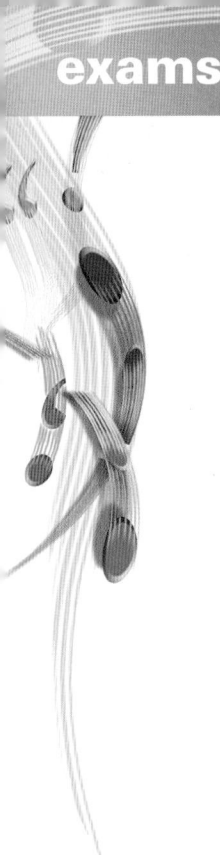
feeling as well as ideas. This feeling is most often expressed through the writer's personal attitudes and points of view. Depending on the subject, you may choose to be angry, cynical, sarcastic, amused and so on.

Loaded words

People might believe they are persuaded by facts and convincing arguments, but advertisers and politicians know that the effect of well-chosen words and phrases is just as important. To return to the subject of smoking in public, a sentence from an argument might read like this:

> It is claimed that a ban on smoking is an infringement of freedom but those who suffer the effects of passive smoking have the right to be free from a risk to their health.

This may be convincing enough for many readers, but to persuade it must be loaded more strongly:

> Those smokers who bleat about the infringement of their freedom have no thoughts for the freedoms of others, as they happily rain down the fumes of death on their neighbours.

Notice that in this context even the word 'neighbours' is loaded because it suggests the idea of good neighbourliness.

How heavily you load your vocabulary will depend on your overall purpose, the subject and the context. If you were concerned about child slavery in the modern world, it would be effective to talk of 'horror', 'despicable cruelty', 'exploitation' and so on, but such language would not be appropriate if you were writing to the school governors about the new school timetable. You might use it, however, if you were writing a tongue-in-cheek piece for a student magazine about school rules.

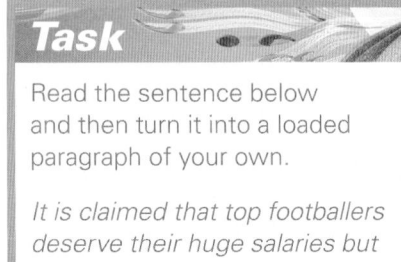

Task

Read the sentence below and then turn it into a loaded paragraph of your own.

It is claimed that top footballers deserve their huge salaries but it is not right that they earn in a week what the country's top surgeons earn in a year.

Task

Write to **persuade** zookeepers of the tremendous benefits of keeping herrings.

Rhetorical questions

You are probably familiar with the device of posing rhetorical questions. They are an appeal to the obvious and the reader's good sense. It is useful to pose a rhetorical question when you want to draw the reader in because you are making a particularly important point. For example, another way of writing the sentence on smoking would be to frame it as a question:

> Can anyone who is concerned with the nation's health support the so-called rights of those who are prepared to rain death on their fellow citizens?

Repetition

Normally you should avoid repeating yourself, but repetition can be used in a special way to drive home a point. A famous example occurred in the speech made by the US civil rights leader Martin Luther King, on 28 August 1963 in Washington DC. If you have studied Ferlinghetti's poem 'Two Scavengers in a Truck, Two Beautiful People in a Mercedes' on page 6 of the AQA *Anthology*, you may have encountered the idea of the American Dream, which is the belief that every North American citizen has the possibility of prospering in a land of freedom. Look at how Luther King plays on the word 'dream' and repeats it to drive home the point that all Americans should be able to share in it, regardless of race.

And so even though we face the difficulties of today and tomorrow, I still have a dream. It is a dream deeply rooted in the American Dream.

I have a dream that one day this nation will rise up and live out the true meaning of its creed: 'We hold these truths to be self-evident; that all men are created equal.'

I have a dream that one day on the red hills of Georgia, the sons of former slaves and the sons of former slave owners will be able to sit down at the table of brotherhood.

I have a dream that one day even the state of Mississippi, a desert state sweltering with the heat of injustice, sweltering with the heat of oppression, will be transformed into an oasis of freedom and justice.

Task

Use three examples of repetition and three rhetorical questions to write the opening paragraph to a **persuasive** piece of writing on the subject of cruelty to animals.

Bold statement

When writing an argument it is important to support your points and not make wild judgements. Persuasive writing is different. Sometimes it is useful to make a bold statement, particularly when you want to stress a key thought. Used sparingly, phrases such as 'It is a fact that...', 'Statistics prove...' and 'Ask anyone in the street...' can be effective. Such phrases suggest that the point of view expressed is indisputable.

Take care not to overdo this technique, however, and there must be a degree of truth in your claim. In other words, you can exaggerate but not lie.

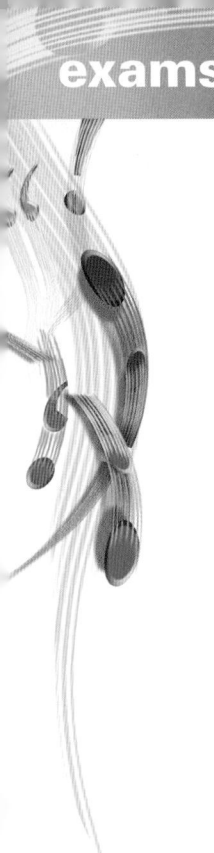

Reinforcing words and phrases

Reinforcing words and phrases include 'of course', 'obviously', 'certainly', 'surely', 'definitely' and 'it goes without saying'. These underline your ideas in such a way as to make it impossible for the audience to disagree with you.

> **Task**
>
> Use three bold statements and three reinforcing words to write the conclusion to an essay entitled 'Saving the planet'.

The rule of threes

Arranging words and phrases into groups of three has a particularly powerful effect on audiences. Mark Antony's 'Friends, Romans, countrymen' in Shakespeare's *Julius Caesar* is a famous example. Politicians are particularly fond of the rule of threes. For example:

...government **of the people**, **by the people**, **for the people**...

Abraham Lincoln

Never in the history of human endeavour has **so much** been owed by **so many** to **so few**.

Winston Churchill

On a less grand scale, you could employ the rule of threes. If you were launching a campaign to replace the school toilets, instead of saying the current facilities are simply 'disgusting', you could write that the toilets are 'dilapidated, disgusting and degrading'. Note that the words in this example also **alliterate**, which rams home the point even further.

Human interest

You may have noticed how newspapers often rely on human stories in their coverage of issues such as law and order, binge drinking, public health and so on. If you can include a particular human example in your discussion of an issue, you can engage the reader's sympathies. For example, to return once more to the issue of smoking, a persuasive article might begin with the story of someone who has suffered the effects of smoking. If you can present a story with which the reader can identify, its impact is even stronger.

> **Task**
>
> **1** Use a human interest story to begin a piece of writing in which you **persuade** the reader that all schools should have a clear policy on bullying.
>
> **2** Recent surveys have shown that every year fewer students are taking up science courses.
>
> Write an article for a student magazine **persuading** the readers that they should consider studying the sciences. You do not need to be a science student yourself to write this article.

Writing to advise

Probably the most familiar examples of writing to advise appear in newspapers and magazines, where it is possible to get advice on everything from what to do when you break up with your boyfriend or girlfriend to how to care for your sick gerbil. The examination will probably concentrate on matters such as giving advice to students, but you can still learn a lot from examples of advice in the media.

Here is a brief piece of advice from a magazine devoted to healthy living:

> **Question: I work at a computer all day. Will this damage my eyes?**
>
> Some studies have suggested heavy computer work could worsen eyesight or increase the risk of cataracts in the long term. In the short term you could end up with eye strain, and staring at a computer encourages less blinking, which means drier eyes. Take a 10 minute screen break every hour, and if you work in an office ask for a health and safety assessment.
>
> *Health Plus*, December 2005

The advice is made up of two parts: first some background information and then an instruction ('Take a 10 minute screen break…'). This example shows that advice can consist of relevant **information** and **direct address** to the reader.

Audience

It is important to consider the audience for which you are writing advice. You must be sensitive to your audience's situation. For instance, if you were asked to provide advice for students on doing part-time work while continuing their studies, it would be a good idea to consider the stress they may encounter as well as the types of job they might do.

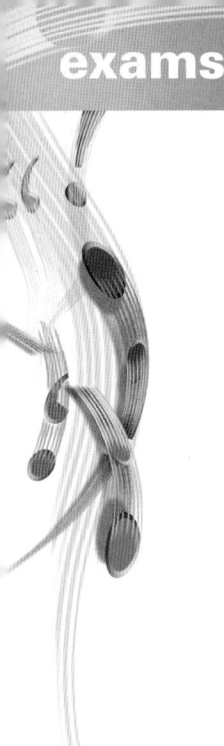

Here is the response to a woman who wrote to a magazine wondering whether she should take out a loan to buy her children presents she cannot afford:

> There's so much pressure to buy things at this time of the year, it's not surprising many of us get into debt. But while the look on your child's face as they open that iPod may seem worth it, it's a short-term pleasure and overspending will lead to long-term problems.
>
> Part of your job as a parent is to teach your children to appreciate the things they do have, rather than hankering after stuff they don't. Whatever your financial situation, you owe it to your kids to say 'No' sometimes.
>
> 'I'd never advocate borrowing on credit cards or store cards for Christmas, no matter how desperate you get,' says Jane Pennington, an independent financial adviser. 'Work out what you can afford, then divide your money into current account (for monthly living costs) and the residual, for holidays and Christmas.'
>
> *Health Plus*, December 2005

The adviser shows sympathy for the woman's emotional situation before giving tough advice. Notice that the writer refers to another authority, the financial adviser. It is often helpful to refer to experts or other cases when giving advice, so as to avoid sounding too bossy or arrogant and to make what you say sound well-informed and authoritative.

Task

Write a letter to a friend who is desperate to overcome a weight problem but cannot resist overeating. Give tactful advice on a healthy diet and exercise etc.

(Sometimes you may need to take the audience's knowledge and experience into special consideration.)

Task

Below are two extracts featuring a power drill. One is aimed at women who are new to do-it-yourself and offers **advice**. The other is written for experienced workers and is more **factual**. Which one is which? How can you tell?

Extract A

Durability and versatility make this 14.4-volt drill/driver a great addition to any toolbox. Handy features include a sensitive electronic switch for a soft start when drilling plus a compact, quick-change battery pack with an easy click locking system. There are no fewer than 16 torque settings and the drill comes with two Ni-Cd batteries.

Extract B

Drills can be corded or cordless, and vary in power. For a good all-rounder, you need a tool that will drill through both wood (for putting on door or cupboard handles, for example) and masonry. The 'hammer' action listed on some drills allows you to drill effectively into a solid wall — for instance, to put up shelves or a hook. Another feature to look out for is a 'keyless chuck'. This means that you don't need a key to unscrew the nozzle to change a drill bit — it has a plastic collar you undo by hand quite easily. This cordless drill is not too heavy, but powerful enough for most jobs.

Language

However good your advice might be, it will not be much use if it is not clear. That is true of any writing, but it is particularly important when giving advice because you have to assume that a person may act on what you have to say. You cannot afford to be confusing.

Here is part of the advice given in a cycling magazine to a 14-year-old wanting to become a professional cyclist:

To achieve your goal you will need to start with some key steps.

First join a 'Go-Ride' club. 'Go-Ride' clubs provide events and coaching for young people. This will make it easier to become active in cycle sport and you will enjoy the social side too.

As for the cycling itself, your pace is directly related to your general fitness. You should take every opportunity to enjoy all sports to improve your basic fitness level. Riding your bike regularly too means improved speed will follow.

When you think you're ready, why not go along to an event and give racing a try?

The next step is to contact your British Cycling Regional Talent Coach to arrange a Talent Team test. Passing this test could gain you a place on the Talent Team — even if you don't get the required result straight away, you will know the level you need to aim for.

Regular club riding will improve your stamina and climbing skills and the club coach should be able to help you with hill- or speed-based training routines so you can further improve your skills.

What kit?

Your bike only needs to be safe and in good working order. There is no need for expensive equipment — remember it is you that provides the power and good bike riding skills.

Cycling clothing is well fitting. The club will have a team strip which you can race in and is good to wear.

Cycling shorts are important, as are mitts and a helmet. Mountain bike-style shoes are ideal to start with as you can race, train and even walk in them and use one set of pedals on all your bikes.

Your nutrition is very important. Don't eat junk food and stick to a well-balanced diet. Drink plenty and eat lots of fruit and you won't go far wrong.

Cycling Plus, July 2005

The adviser has assumed that the 14-year-old knows nothing or very little about what to do. Since the young person is already enthusiastic, there is no need to do more than provide advice in the form of useful information.

Most importantly, the advice is **organised** along **step-by-step** lines. These steps are shown by the highlighted sections. The last paragraph, about kit, goes through the requirements topic by topic. In other words, the advice is systematic. This is a simple approach but a clear and useful way of organising a wide range of advice. Jumping back and forth from one area to another is confusing.

Note that although the advice is largely factual and could be useful to anybody wanting to take up cycle racing, the writer uses the personal 'you'. Even if you don't know whom you are addressing personally, it is always useful to write your advice as if to an individual. This book, for example, addresses 'you', rather than a vague, unmentioned audience.

It is important to choose language to **suit the audience**. The language you might use when writing for children would not be suitable for an adult audience. In the examination you may be asked to write for people of your own age, but you could equally be required to write for people who are not in your age group.

> **Remember:** once again, the words, purpose and audience are vital.

Task

Read the two extracts taken from government pamphlets on keeping warm in the winter. Extract 1 is aimed at the general public. Extract 2 is written for people with learning disabilities. The information in each is slightly different.

Combine the two sets of information to produce a single pamphlet for either the general public or people with learning disabilities. You may need to rearrange the information and add some of your own.

Task

Many adults are suspicious of young people who hang around the streets and sometimes become a bit rowdy.

Write a leaflet for a local community group, **explaining** what young people really feel and giving **advice** on how the neighbourhood should treat young people.

1

Why keeping warm matters

To keep well during winter, it's essential to keep warm. As the weather gets colder, we are all more likely to catch colds or flu; and if your body temperature drops then the risks of a heart attack, stroke or breathing difficulties increase. This is especially true for older people, or if you have a chronic disease, or are vulnerable due to physical disability.

So the best way to combat winter is to keep warm and follow as healthy a lifestyle as possible. What you eat and drink, and the exercise you take, can make a big difference. And, as part of keeping well, it's vital to keep your home warm and keep yourself warm when you go out.

This booklet has advice on how to keep warm and well this winter. Many of the suggestions are common sense, but are still important to remember. And you may find some practical ideas and useful information that are new to you. There is news of:

- more help for people aged 60 or over — a £200 winter fuel payment to help towards the cost of keeping your home warm

- extra help for fitting insulation or even a new central heating system in your home.

2

If you have any questions about keeping warm and well, call the winter **warmth advice line** on 0800 085 7000.
It is staffed by people who should be able to answer your questions ... or put you in touch with someone in your area who will be able to help. There will be an interpreter to provide advice in your own language if you need this.
Your call is free.

keep well

3

WINTER WARMTH ADVICE LINE
8am to 8pm Monday to Friday

FREEPHONE 0800 085 7000
TEXTPHONE 0800 085 7857

'Keep Warm, Keep Well, A Winter Guide 2004–05'

2

Keep warm, dress well

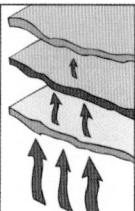

Wear the kind of clothes that keep you warm and help stop you getting ill.

At home

Wear thin clothes on top of each other instead of one thick jumper or jacket.

Warm air gets held between layers.

Choose wool, cotton or light fleecy clothes.

When it's very, very cold, a good way to keep warm in bed is to wear woolly socks + woolly hat or head scarf + warm night-dress or pyjamas + thermal underwear

Outdoors

 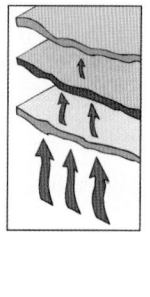

Wear thin clothes on top of each other under a coat. This will keep you warmer than a thick jumper or jacket.

Wear a hat or cap or you'll get very cold very quickly.

Wear warm, dry, flat shoes or boots. The soles should not be smooth. Then you won't slip when it's icy.

6

7

Winter Warmth Advice Line
8am to 8pm Monday to Friday

Freephone 0800 085 7000
Textphone 0800 085 7857

'Keep Warm, Keep Well, A Winter Guide for People with Learning Disabilities 2004–05'

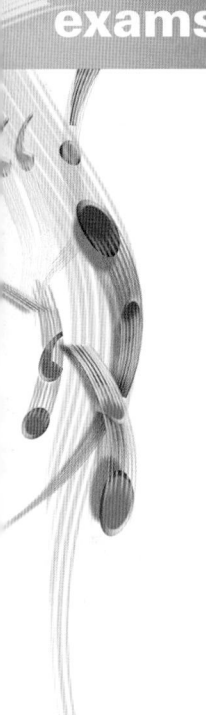

Task

Entering school or college for the first time can be a daunting or even frightening experience.

Write a guide for new entrants to your school or college. You should **inform** them about the important rules and facilities and **advise** them on how best to settle in.

Remember, you might write differently for an 11-year-old entering a school than for a student entering a college.

Task

Energy conservation is very much in the news.

Write a letter to your head and governors **advising** them on how your school or college could save energy and become environmentally friendly.

English
Paper 2 Section A

Reading response to poetry
from different cultures

Your AQA *Anthology* includes a section containing poems from different cultures. Part of your written examination for English requires you to respond to these poems. The skills needed to write about poetry are covered in Chapter 2 of this book. The extra requirement of Paper 2 Section A is that you compare the poems as well as write about them individually.

> **Remember:**
> if you refer to the English Literature poems by mistake, you will get no marks.

Choosing and organising the poems

Stage 1

In the examination you will be asked to compare the elements of two poems. No matter what the poems are, the skills for comparing them are the same.

The first thing you need to do is think about what comparing poems actually means in practical terms. Will you be comparing language, themes or the ways that writers deal with different cultures? The answer is that you could be asked to do any of those things and more besides. Trying to predict the question you might be asked is not a good strategy for achieving success in the exam. If the question you have prepared does not appear on the exam paper, you might be thrown into a panic and end up giving a bad impression of your abilities.

That said, there are only so many elements you could be asked to compare. Looking through past papers with your teacher should help you to identify the types of comparison that are asked for. The typical areas of comparison are:

* Language — how does the poet choose words for effect?
* Theme — what are the central ideas of the poem?
* Feelings and emotions — what sentiments is the poet trying to get across?
* Cultures and traditions — how are these represented by the poet?
* Presentation — how is the poem laid out on the page?

Below is a list of the poems from different cultures in the AQA *Anthology*. Copy out the table and complete it as you explore the poems in class. (It is not expected that you will necessarily cover all of the poems with your teacher.) The first poem has been done for you.

Poem	Feature 1	Feature 2	Feature 3
'Limbo'	Unusual presentation	Repetition	Cultures — slavery
'Nothing's Changed'			
'Island Man'			
'Blessing'			
'Two Scavengers in a Truck…'			
'Night of the Scorpion'			
'Vultures'			
'What Were They Like?'			
from 'Search For My Tongue'			
from 'Unrelated Incidents'			
'Half-Caste'			
'Love After Love'			
'This Room'			
'Not My Business'			
'Presents from my Aunts in Pakistan'			
'Hurricane Hits England'			

Features	Poems
Political and social comment	'Nothing's Changed' 'Two Scavengers in a Truck' 'Vultures' 'Unrelated Incidents' 'Not My Business'
Sense of place	'Nothing's Changed' 'Night of the Scorpion' 'Island Man' 'Blessing' 'Two Scavengers in a Truck' 'Hurricane Hits England'
Repetition	'Limbo' 'Night of the Scorpion' 'Half-Caste' 'Not My Business'
Unusual presentation	'Limbo' 'Search For My Tongue' 'Unrelated Incidents'

As you work through the poems in class you should note which ones can sensibly be linked together. It is then a good idea to reorganise the poems into groups according to the particular features they share. This could take the form of a table such as the one on the left.

There are more categories than this and you should consult your teacher about elements the poems have in common. Once you have added all the categories you will have a useful preparation tool which you can add to as you go through the course.

Note: for the purpose of comparison, one poem might appear in more than one grouping.

Culture

One element you might have to comment on in the exam is how the different poems talk about **culture**. To do this you need a clear idea of what the word 'culture' could mean. It could be connected with any of the following, and many more:

* race
* religious attitude
* literature
* entertainment
* politics
* education
* social behaviour
* nationality
* customs
* music
* shopping
* food
* wealth
* language
* traditions
* painting
* place
* dress
* poverty

Task

Design a table with the cultural factors listed above down the left-hand side. Across the top of the table write the names of the poems you have studied (one column for each poem). In each box you have created, say how the poem comments on the aspects of culture relevant to it.

You should not try to write everything you know about a poem if it does not suit the question. For example, there is no need to comment on the unusual presentation of 'Limbo' if you have been asked about culture.

Stage 2

Next you need to look at the ways in which you might explore the poems in the examination.

Read 'Nothing's Changed' from page 6 of the AQA *Anthology*. The first question you should ask yourself is: 'What is the poem about?' Your first impression might be that it is a story about a man who goes back to District Six and sees how it has changed. That is the literal meaning, but you need to consider what the poet is really telling you. You could make some simple comments on this in a few lines, picking out such ideas as:

❋ injustice   ❋ prejudice   ❋ life under apartheid   ❋ rich vs poor

Task

1 Write a paragraph explaining what you think the poem 'Nothing's Changed' is about.

2 Now take the ideas from the paragraph you have just written and expand on them. Write a two-page essay on the main themes in 'Nothing's Changed'.

Once you have decided what the general message of the poem is, you should begin to think in more detail about what you might say.

Ladder of skills

Your examination answers will be marked using a document called a mark scheme. It is more helpful to think of a mark scheme as a ladder of skills.

Grade A*/A	❋ Sees the concepts involved in the poems.
	❋ Close analysis of poems, references integrated with argument.
	❋ Consistent insight and convincing/imaginative interpretation.
	❋ Analysis of a variety of the poet's techniques.
	❋ Exploration of an empathy with feelings, attitudes and ideas.
	❋ Sophisticated and convincing use of critical terms to describe the concepts.
Grade B/C	❋ Clear/competent discussion of poems, including effective use of textual detail.
	❋ Structured response which selects and comments on different aspects of poems.
	❋ Understanding of feelings, attitudes and ideas.
	❋ Some appropriate use of specialist terms.
Grade D/E	❋ Tends to paraphrase the poems.
	❋ Response is largely descriptive, but some comment on effects achieved by the poet.
	❋ Awareness of feelings, attitudes and ideas.
	❋ Repeats what the poet says without explaining why it has been said.

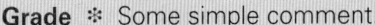
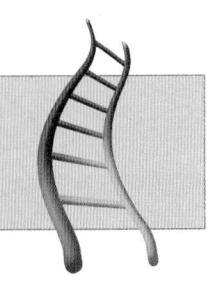

Grade ❋ Some simple comment.
F/G ❋ Answer is mainly narrative.
     ❋ General/descriptive comment — some relevant detail.
     ❋ Simple comments on some aspects of presentation.

Commenting on language

Remember that the best answers don't simply look at the story the poem is telling, but comment on the poem as a piece of writing. They make it clear that the poet has made definite choices of words to produce certain effects.

You should know the poems thoroughly before you go into the exam. If, for example, you were asked to comment on the opening of 'Nothing's Changed', you might select a few key points from the opening stanza that show how the poet is trying to manipulate the reader. Examples of such points are given below for stanzas 1 and 3:

Small round hard stones click ——— *All of the words are monosyllabic (this makes it sound harsh)*

under my heels,

seeding grasses thrust

bearded seeds

into trouser cuffs, cans, ——— *Man-made litter spoils the area*

trodden on, crunch

in tall, purple-flowering,

amiable weeds. ——— *Why are the weeds amiable?*

Brash with glass, ——— *The glass does not belong*

name flaring like a flag,

it squats ——— *Menacing, unpleasant*

in the grass and weeds,

incipient Port Jackson trees:

new, up-market, haute cuisine,

guard at the gatepost, ——— *Guards at a restaurant?*

whites only inn. ——— *Pun on 'inn' and 'in'*

Do not try to comment on every line: this would lead to a simple list, wasting what little exam time you have and earning few marks. The notes above are based on only two stanzas, yet they include a good deal of high-level language analysis.

Connotation is particularly important when commenting on language; think about the word 'brash' in stanza 3, for instance. Look back at the notes on connotation in Section 1 (pages 47–50).

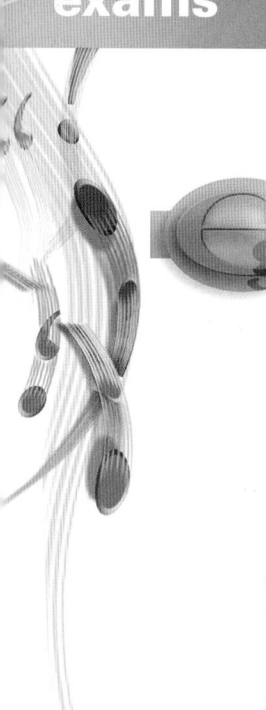

Examples of student performance

Consider the following question:

How does the poet get across his ideas in the poem 'Nothing's Changed'?

Grade-E–G answer

The poem is about the black people and the white people in South Africa. The black people are poor and the white people are rich. The poet is standing outside a restaurant but they won't let him in because he is black and only white people can go in. The place is not very nice because there is rubbish and weeds.

Examiner's comment

This is a series of simple comments on the basic message of the poem. The comments are brief and undeveloped and there is no support for what is said. There is some general awareness of the content of the poem.

Grade-C answer

The poet is angry because the poor black people are not allowed in the restaurant. The restaurant is a place which is a 'Whites only inn' and this makes the poet angry because he has lived there and thinks he should have the right to go in as well. The landscape is important because it shows that nature is taking back the land.

Examiner's comment

The candidate grasps the emotion of anger in the poem. The comments have some support and a reason for the poet's anger is explored briefly. The answer then moves on to the use of the landscape, showing that the candidate also has an understanding of the idea that nature is against the restaurant.

Grade-A answer

The first line consists entirely of monosyllabic words. This is not a normal pattern of speech. This unusual word combination has been chosen with a clear purpose in mind — to make the place that is being introduced seem harsh and unfriendly. The whole message of the poem is that some people are not allowed to join in with the good life in South Africa.

Examiner's comment

The answer begins with a strong comment on the poet's use of language. The candidate recognises that the unusual word pattern has been chosen deliberately in order to create an effect. He then goes on to suggest that the poem has a clear message.

Comparing poems

In the exam you will not be writing about one poem on its own but will be asked to compare two poems. With this in mind, read the task and student responses that follow. This is designed to prepare you for writing about poetry in the English exam.

Compare 'Nothing's Changed' with another poem that deals with contrast between two worlds.

This is a standard exam-style question. First you must decide which other poem to use. If you have completed the earlier exercises in this chapter you will have a detailed table of which poems work best together, and you should see clearly which poems also feature contrasting worlds.

For the purpose of illustrating how you might approach this question, the second poem chosen here is 'Two Scavengers in a Truck, Two Beautiful People in a Mercedes' from page 8 of the AQA *Anthology*.

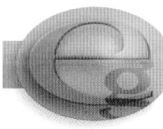

Examples of student performance

Grade-F answer

The poem 'Nothing's Changed' has a man who is poor and he is outside a restaurant. It is a restaurant for rich people and only for white people. In 'Two Scavengers...' there are poor people on the garbage truck and rich people in the Mercedes. This poem is also about rich and poor and how they are different.

Examiner's comment

The Grade-F approach to the question is a basic list of actions and obvious features from the two poems. By now you should be able to predict how a Grade-C answer will differ from this answer. At Grade C there will be more of an overview of the poems and an understanding of the feelings and emotions involved.

Grade-C answer

Both 'Nothing's Changed' and 'Two Scavengers...' are about different worlds. Both poems show that people can be angry about the way lives are different just because one person has money or has different coloured skin.

The appearance of the 'whites only inn' makes the poet angry. His anger is shown when he says things like 'Hands burn/for a stone, a bomb'.

Examiner's comment

This answer shows that the candidate appreciates there are ideas common to both poems. The candidate goes on to identify the source of the poet's anger in 'Nothing's Changed' and how it is shown with an appropriate quotation. She should then treat the other poem in a similar way.

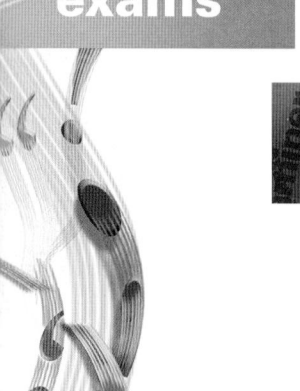

At Grade A the answer will focus in detail on one or two main aspects of the poem. The Grade-A candidate knows that the poems are contrasting two worlds for a reason and will not simply pick out parts of the storyline.

Grade-A answer

'Nothing's Changed' and 'Two Scavengers...' both reflect societies in which injustice is deeply rooted. These two poems do this in order to make the reader think about the kind of unfairness that is found in the world, no matter where you live. The central focus is the divide between rich and poor, which is heightened in 'Nothing's Changed' by racial prejudice. Both poems also expose the hypocrisy of modern societies. Apartheid has finished but there is still a 'Whites only inn'. The American dream assures that 'everything is always possible', yet there is still a 'gulf/in the high seas/of this democracy'.

Examiner's comment

The starting-point for this answer is an idea shared by both poems. This is illustrated and highlighted by brief but precise quotation. Obviously a full answer would need to continue with more explanation of the exact circumstances, but this candidate grasps the idea that each poet is trying to get across a central message.

A Grade-A candidate should be capable of concentrating on the ideas and will be able to move easily from one poem to the other throughout the answer and so **integrate comments**. This is a high-order skill, however, and you must be careful not to become muddled.

As you prepare to write about poetry in the English exam, try to apply the techniques that have been covered in this section and in chapter 2 on responding to literature. Once you have the skills, you can apply them to any poetry question. The better you know the poems the easier it is to write about them. Keep reading the poems throughout your GCSE course and you should find that you become more confident in writing about them.

English
Paper 2 Section B

Writing to inform, explain and describe

Although they appear as separate tasks in Paper 2, informing and explaining are similar activities. They both involve setting out information clearly, but for different purposes:

* **Writing to inform** is just that. It sets out facts and other information in a clear and organised way. The aim is to present what **information** the reader **needs to know**.
* **Writing to explain** also aims to provide clear information, but it must be combined with **reasons**.

For example, the weather forecast is pure information, but saying why certain parts of the Caribbean and the USA suffer so many hurricanes is explanation.

How much do you know about the work of the charity Age Concern? Probably not much, unless you know somebody who is involved. The leaflet reproduced on page 134 **informs** the reader about the charity — the primary purpose of the writing is to provide facts in a clear way.

Of course, you will know from your study of media texts that the picture of the smiling elderly lady is more than a plain fact; it suggests that Age Concern brings happiness to its clients.

Task

Leaflet A is written in note form for immediate impact. Using the facts in the leaflet, write a short article on what Age Concern does. You should use connecting words and phrases, such as 'first'/'second', 'in addition', 'what is more', 'finally' etc. You will also need to include suitable verbs, such as 'Age Concern **provides**...' and so on.

Leaflet A   **Side 1**   **Side 2**

All You Need to Know

We work to promote the well-being of all older people in the country, by providing services and campaigning on issues that affect the quality of later life.

Advocacy — independent and trustworthy support for older people facing problems.

Benefits Advice — benefit checks, help completing claim forms and representation at tribunals.

Day Centres — over 40 centres in the county offer a friendly day out and a hot meal for frail older people.

Help at Home — funded by Shropshire County Council — domestic help and volunteer visiting to help older people stay in their own home.

Home from Hospital — volunteers visit older people leaving hospital to help with non-medical tasks.

Home Visiting — volunteers befriend older people at home.

Information — expertise, fact sheets and a free A–Z of Services.

Insurance — competitively priced for people over 50 for travel, property etc.

AGE *Concern*   Shropshire Telford & Wrekin

Leisure Activities — including the annual Afternoon of Entertainment and, in alternate years, a Handicraft Exhibition and a Literary Competition.

Living Well — classes in gentle exercise and movement and Tai Chi funded by the Community Fund.

Neighbourhood Contact — in parts of Telford older people are given help and support to expand their social circle.

North East Shropshire Rehabilitation Team (NESrT) — volunteers work within a professional team to provide non-medical support to older clients during six-week intensive rehabilitation.

Parish Links — volunteers, within Shropshire, act as links between Age Concern and their community.

Pub Clubs — luncheon clubs in Shropshire give older people a chance to get out and meet people.

If you would like to know more:

Age Concern Shropshire
Telford & Wrekin

Head Office in Shrewsbury
01743 233123
acinfo@btconnect.com

Age Concern South Shropshire
01584 876039

Age Concern Whitchurch
01948 665317

Age Concern Wrekin
01952 293500

'All our services rely on volunteers and are supported by fundraising. Invest in your future by helping Age Concern now!'

A free leaflet "Leaving Money to Age Concern in Your Will" is available on request.

Charity No 1090445

As well as providing information, Age Concern wants to interest people in its activities, so Leaflet B goes a little further by **explaining** what it is like to be a volunteer. The piece is still made up of mainly factual **information**, but this is presented in such a way as to give something of the flavour of volunteer work. It also briefly **explains** how to apply.

An important difference between the two leaflets is that Leaflet A is written for a general audience, while Leaflet B is aimed directly at possible volunteers. Notice the use of you/your.

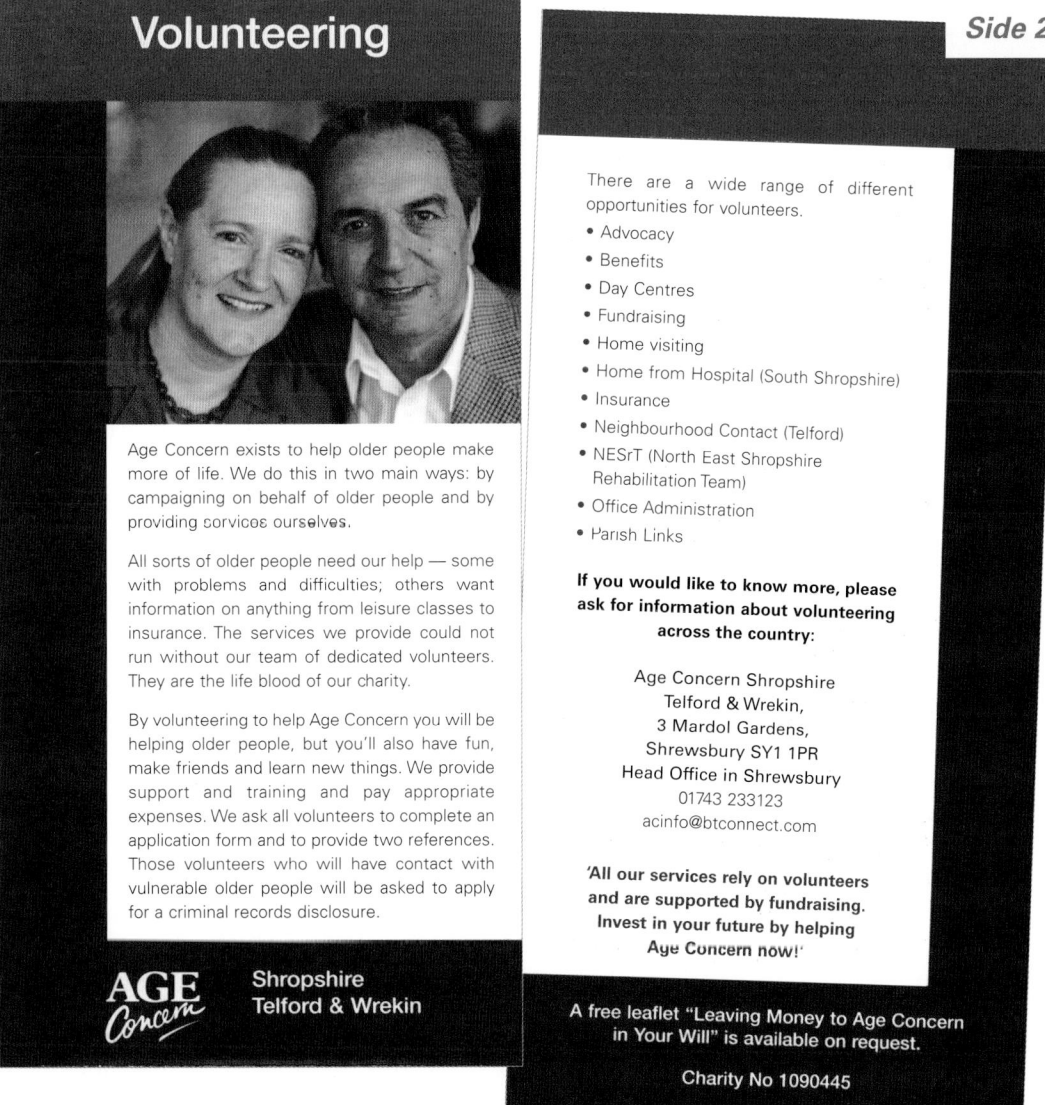

Leaflet B   **Side 1**

Volunteering

Age Concern exists to help older people make more of life. We do this in two main ways: by campaigning on behalf of older people and by providing services ourselves.

All sorts of older people need our help — some with problems and difficulties; others want information on anything from leisure classes to insurance. The services we provide could not run without our team of dedicated volunteers. They are the life blood of our charity.

By volunteering to help Age Concern you will be helping older people, but you'll also have fun, make friends and learn new things. We provide support and training and pay appropriate expenses. We ask all volunteers to complete an application form and to provide two references. Those volunteers who will have contact with vulnerable older people will be asked to apply for a criminal records disclosure.

AGE *Concern*   Shropshire Telford & Wrekin

Side 2

There are a wide range of different opportunities for volunteers.

- Advocacy
- Benefits
- Day Centres
- Fundraising
- Home visiting
- Home from Hospital (South Shropshire)
- Insurance
- Neighbourhood Contact (Telford)
- NESrT (North East Shropshire Rehabilitation Team)
- Office Administration
- Parish Links

If you would like to know more, please ask for information about volunteering across the country:

Age Concern Shropshire
Telford & Wrekin,
3 Mardol Gardens,
Shrewsbury SY1 1PR
Head Office in Shrewsbury
01743 233123
acinfo@btconnect.com

'**All our services rely on volunteers and are supported by fundraising. Invest in your future by helping Age Concern now!**'

A free leaflet "Leaving Money to Age Concern in Your Will" is available on request.

Charity No 1090445

Organisation

The first Assessment Objective for writing requires that you write clearly. To make sure your writing to inform and explain is clear, it must be properly organised.

Read this passage by a student completing a task to inform a parent–teacher association of improvements that could be made to his school:

The toilets are terrible. There's no toilet paper and it's not healthy to have greasy chips every day. Sixty per cent of pupils say they should eat healthy salads but the

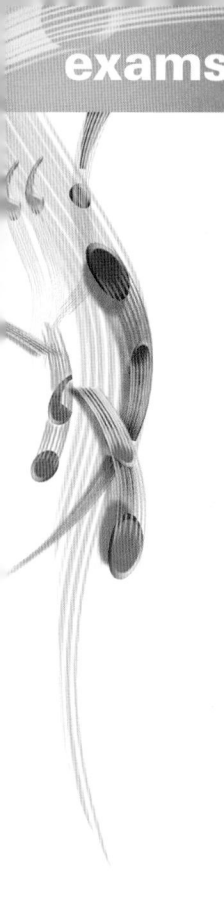

machines only serve fizzy drinks. Also the sports hall is very old and the changing rooms are dilapidated. Sport is very essential. There should be more time on the timetable for football and other sports. I think we should have a longer lunch hour. We have no time to relax and we have to rush back to lessons and they say you can't concentrate if you are tired.

There's plenty of useful information in the passage and the sentences are clear. There's some evidence of deliberate vocabulary choice (e.g. 'healthy', 'dilapidated', 'essential'), but the information is presented like a list of thoughts that pop up in the student's mind, more or less at random. As such, the student is writing at about Grade-F level.

We can improve the student's grade simply by organising and linking the ideas more effectively:

First there is the issue of the toilets, which are a disgrace. They are positively unhealthy and we are not even provided with toilet paper.

Second, despite the fact that 60% of our pupils think that the school should encourage healthier eating by providing salads, we are still served up greasy chips every day. What is more, the drinks machines only deliver fizzy drinks.

Futhermore, even if the school served healthier food, we barely have time to eat it because the lunch break is so short. We have no time to relax, so that our powers of concentration must suffer during the afternoon.

Finally, still on health matters, too little time is devoted to sports, which are so essential to our wellbeing, and the problem is made worse by the dilapidated state of the sports hall.

The most important feature of this version is that the ideas are organised and sequenced with clear **signposts** (indicated in yellow). Related information is organised into **paragraphs** and some words are used to link the details to a more general concern. These are indicated in pink.

A full answer would involve much more detail, but students who take care to **connect** their ideas in this way would be eligible for a Grade C and upwards. The effective use of paragraphs alone moves the writing into the D/C zone.

An important aspect of writing to explain is that you may have to give **reasons** for such things as particular actions or choices. For example, consider the following task.

Task

Write an article in which you **explain** why you enjoy a particular leisure activity.

Of course, whatever activity we are interested in — whether it is rock climbing, playing the trumpet, attending dance classes or even lying on a beach — it is likely that we do it because it gives us pleasure. Unfortunately, however much you might enjoy martial arts, for example, simply to say so is not a reason for anyone else to take an interest. When you are explaining, you must put yourself in the reader's shoes. Ask yourself, 'I know why, but will the reader understand why?'

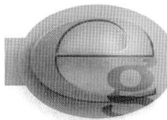

Examples of student performance

Here are three attempts at the task by a student who is obviously keen on photography:

Attempt 1

Photography is my passion. I belong to a local camera club and we go out every weekend. Last week we went up to the Yorkshire Moors and I took some great pictures of the sunset. I've also taken lots of pictures on holiday. There are some fantastic scenes in the Canary Islands and I've made my pictures into a slide show, which I've shown at the club. I was told how good they are and some of my pictures are on display.

Examiner's comment

The candidate starts well by stating that photography is his 'passion' and he uses several words — 'great', 'fantastic', 'good' — that hint at some enthusiasm for the subject, but the writing is mainly a list of activities. The information is relevant but no detailed *reasons* are given as to why any of it should be interesting. Simply saying that his pictures are great does not convince the reader that they really are. This attempt would receive a Grade D/E.

Attempt 2

Photography is my passion and I have sought to develop my skills by joining a local camera club. Every weekend we go somewhere in search of new and interesting pictures. Last week we went up to the Yorkshire Moors and I succeeded in capturing the magic of the scene at sunset.

Of course, I've also taken lots of pictures on holiday. The Canary Islands offer some wonderful opportunities for the photographer and I gained real satisfaction in turning my pictures into a slide show, which I've shown at the club. I was thrilled when I was praised for my work, especially now that some of my pictures are on public display.

Examiner's comment

In this attempt the candidate gives more detail about his hobby and identifies some of its aspects, e.g. 'develop skills', 'new', 'interesting', 'capturing the magic', 'real satisfaction', 'turning pictures into a slide show', 'thrilled'. The reader can appreciate that the candidate enjoys his hobby.

However, although the candidate reflects a good range of his feelings and *what* he enjoys, he still does not explain *why*. Although there is more variety, the structure still resembles a list. This attempt would merit a Grade C.

Attempt 3

Photography is my passion because there is so much satisfaction to be gained from creating something inventive, beautiful or even strange. Some people might

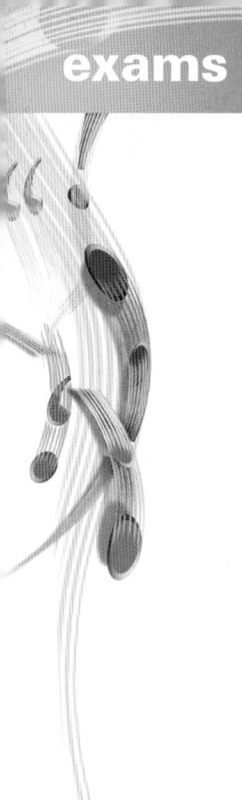

say all you have to do is point the camera and shoot. There is much more to photography than that.

Apart from the technical side, which I find fascinating, you need a good eye and every subject is a challenge. For instance, last week our camera club went to the Yorkshire Moors. Most of the day, I struggled to take a decent shot. Then, at the end of the day, the setting sun cast a wonderful light across the landscape and I was so thrilled when I found that I had captured the essence of the scene in my pictures.

I also enjoy photography because I can give others pleasure. There was such a buzz around the camera club after my slide show of pictures from my holiday in the Canaries and I feel so proud every time I see my photographs, which are now on public display.

Examiner's comment

In this attempt the candidate has used some of his experiences to **illustrate** aspects of his feelings towards photography. He has identified clearly a range of reasons why he enjoys his hobby: 'satisfaction', 'creating something inventive', 'technical side...fascinating', 'good eye', 'wonderful light', 'thrilled', 'captured the essence', 'give others pleasure', 'buzz', 'proud'.

The candidate has integrated facts, thoughts and feelings and put the task of explaining at the centre of his writing, so there is no sense of a mechanical list. This would gain a Grade A.

Task

There is increasing concern about cheating in coursework, whether it be downloading ready-made essays from the internet or parents helping their children too much.

Write a letter to a local newspaper that has reported a case of cheating in a local school, informing the readers what the problem is and **explaining** how it should be tackled.

Writing to describe

Go into any library or bookshop and you will find fictional and non-fictional writing of all kinds, often divided into sections such as romance, mystery, science fiction, history, travel, biography and so on, but you will not find any shelf devoted to descriptive writing. However, look a little closer and you will find descriptive writing everywhere, not just in the fiction section.

In Paper 2 Section B you are usually asked to describe a place or a vivid situation or scene. For example, you might be asked to describe a busy station or what a photograph suggests to you. Below are six extracts from different sources. All contain descriptive writing.

8

Extract 1: 'Country File' article

This is the nearest of the six extracts to pure description and is taken from a regular newspaper column.

After some rain, the woods release that unmistakable autumn fragrance. The smell of rotting leaves and damp earth may be enhanced by the release of millions of fungal spores, but the scent is intoxicatingly beery with a pungency that wafts back through years of memory to the autumn woods of childhood.

This fragrance is an archive of decay and decomposition; the return of life to the soil; a marker of the restorative nature of death. If this scent had a colour, it would be a yellow ochre, bronze and chocolate of hazel, hawthorn and lime leaves. If it had a form, it would be of a shadowy figure slipping through the trees. If it had a sound, it would be a deep murmuring carried by trickling streams. The woods are quiet, except for groups of small birds fossicking through the branches and the mew of buzzards overhead.

Paul Evans, *Guardian*, 26 October 2005

The writing is full of vocabulary that relates to our senses in some way. Notice that in the first paragraph the descriptive words are not scattered at random but grouped so as to focus the reader's attention on a single sensation. It is important that the vocabulary is concentrated and does not introduce different or jarring associations.

Task

The basic idea of the first paragraph is that after rain in the autumn you can smell rotting leaves — not an agreeable-sounding sensation.

What particular words does the author use to make the sensation seem attractive?

Task

Write a paragraph about one of the following:
* an empty football stadium
* a street strewn with litter
* a supermarket car park

Use some concentrated vocabulary to make the scene appear interesting but not necessarily attractive. Imagine you are standing absolutely still in the place.

In the second paragraph the writer broadens the scope of his description by linking the smells of the wood to other sensations, and introduces hints of sound and movement. Notice the use of repetition, which provides variation in the sentence structures. Remember, if you use the same sentence shape over and over again your writing will become monotonous.

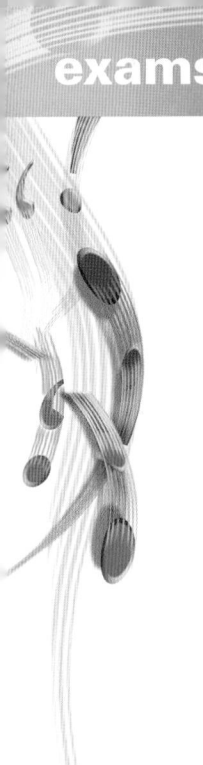
Extract 2: Student answer

The first extract relies on a rich choice of vocabulary and recognisably descriptive words. This method is not as easy as it appears, however, as can be seen from the following student's work:

> I love to lie on the soft sand on an island in the middle of nowhere, with the waves gently crashing and the sun beating down and making everything shine like a neon light in the sky.
>
> I run my finger through the fluffy sand and birds fly overhead and then I walk towards the sparkling sea, where fish are splashing about. I listen to all the sounds and I can feel the light breeze on my face as the sun beats down and the wind slowly passes through the trees just in front of me. I walk towards the quaint green trees and the beautiful flowers and there is a wonderful feeling all around me.

The student is obviously aware of the need to describe, and chooses some descriptive vocabulary and makes a clear comparison. The vocabulary is thoughtlessly chosen, however. Is sand really 'fluffy'? Is it possible for the sea to 'gently crash'? And what are 'quaint green trees'? There are a few words that stand out, but most are obvious or weak: 'sparkling sea', 'light breeze', 'sun beating down', 'beautiful flowers'. The one original comparison, 'like a neon light in the sky', is awkward and the exact meaning of the sentence has not been thought through. Unfortunately, a number of students write in this way and even those who are better writers occasionally slip into the thoughtless use of 'colourful' words for their own sake.

Extract 3: Short story

That evening he strolled towards the main square. It felt like a different town: boys with adult faces and crewcuts were selling nuts in twists of paper; teenage girls paraded up and down, arms linked, cheeks sucked in; old men watched from the blotchy walls of bars, their foreheads creased by a lifetime of hats. Dusk came down so fast, you could almost see the sky change. It made you want to walk with your head tilted back.

Rupert Thompson, 'No Girl'

> See the comments on adjectives and adverbs (pages 62–63).

This third extract is from a short story. It contains few obviously colourful words.

The important quality of this description is its **sense of place**, which is created by isolating key details and letting them speak for themselves. The focus is on the people in the little town, but the author does not attempt to describe them in detail. Instead, he picks out those features we might remember if we had visited the place: the 'boys with adult faces', the 'teenage girls paraded' (why not simply 'walked'?), the 'old men watched', the 'lifetime of hats'. The only obviously descriptive adjective is 'blotchy', but because it stands on its own the effect is vivid.

Ask yourself how you know the place being described isn't Blackpool.

Task

Write a single paragraph describing your school ground at break, seen through the eyes of a person from another country.

Extract 4: Novel

An important skill in any kind of descriptive writing is to see things with a fresh eye. Extracts 4 and 5 involve visitors to new places. We tend to take familiar places for granted and probably do not look at them closely. When we visit a strange place for the first time we are more alert.

The following extract comes from a novel. In this scene the main character, a well-educated black English woman, arrives in Jamaica. This is the first time she has visited a non-white society.

> As we drove into Kingston I sat back in my seat and I looked out of the window. It was dark. Down in the midst of the jewel I had seen from the air, palm trees swayed. Their thick trunks loomed over us in the moonlight, like giants' legs waiting at the side of the road. Then along the streets the shacks began to appear. The buildings had no details in the night light except where a small fire showed up their flimsy wooden construction or a streetlight cast a glow over the scene. Black people were everywhere. Sitting by the shacks, walking along the road, in the road, standing, talking, gesturing in conversation, calling across to others. Eating food, watching the traffic going by. Bending over to small children. Children that ran and played, darting around in a game.
>
> Andrea Levy, *Fruit of the Lemon*, 1999

There are many features in this passage that could be examined and which would be helpful in your own descriptive writing. Three stand out:

1 Structure. Although the extract is quite short, there is a sense of movement, literally from the airport into the town and also from darkness into a kind of light. The viewpoint is consistent with peering out of a car window trying to make out what the place is like.

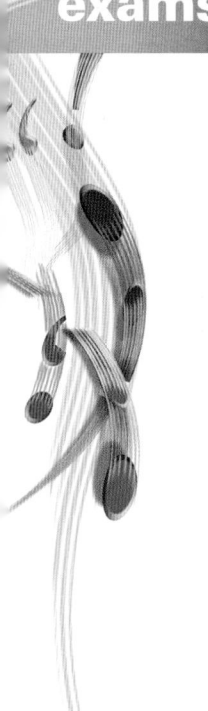

2 **Vocabulary and imagery**. Descriptive words are carefully rationed. The use of 'loomed' and the single simile in the passage, 'like giants' legs', stand out partly because we do not normally think of palm trees as threatening.

3 **Grammar**. Towards the end of the extract the author uses a succession of participles (words ending in '-ing'). They introduce a feeling of continuous movement and activity. If the writer had used the more usual past tense the effect would have been much flatter:

Black people were everywhere. They sat by the shacks, walked along the road, in the road, stood, talked, gestured in conversation, called across to others. Ate food, watched the traffic go by. Bent over to small children. Children that ran and played, darted around in a game.

Extract 5: Travel book

This extract from a travel book describes what the author sees from a train in Japan.

I looked out the window, watching for the Tokyo suburbs to end, but they continued to appear, stretching as far as I could see along the flat biscuit-brown plain. The Hikari Super Express, the fastest passenger train in the world, which travels over 300 miles from Tokyo to Kyoto in less than three hours, never really leaves the pure horror of the megalopolis that joins these two cities. Under a sky, which tawny fumes have given the texture of wool, are pylons secured by cables, buildings shaped like jumbo rheostats and an unzoned clutter of houses, none larger than two stories, whose picture windows front on to factories. Inside — I knew this from an evening visit in Tokyo — the houses are stark, austere, impeccable, impossible to date accurately; outside the faded wood retains the colour of soot that has sifted from the neighbourhood factory chimney, and no house is more than a foot from the one next door. To see this population density is to conclude that overcrowding requires good manners; any disturbance, anything less than perfect order, would send it sprawling.

Paul Theroux, *The Great Railway Bazaar*, 1975

Task

Pick out what you consider to be some of the key features of Extract 5. Arrange your choices into types, such as nouns, adjectives, comparisons etc.

Task

Write a descriptive account of arriving in a strange place for the first time, using some of the techniques in Extracts 4 and 5.

Extract 6: Cookery writing

Some students think descriptive writing is about making things seem pretty. The important point is to convey **interest** in what you describe. The student who described the beach in Extract 2 wasn't really interested in the subject.

The following piece of descriptive writing is taken from a cookery book called *A Taste of India* (1985). The author, Madhur Jaffrey, travelled through India and wrote an account of places and their local dishes. In this extract the cookery angle is clear from the references to various delicacies, such as sharbats and khas roots, but notice how Jaffrey provides a framework for introducing the dishes. She presents a picture of faded glory, of an upper-class family struggling to maintain its traditions of courtesy and hospitality.

Jaffrey does this by selecting **significant details**. She doesn't attempt to describe everything but **selects** those features that help to build up the image she wants to convey.

The mansion needs paint. Its ochre wash, done perhaps twenty or thirty years ago, is now stained with the drippings of as many monsoons. Gardeners have long since abandoned the grounds — only a few determined weeds stick out of the hard, caked earth. A curtain — a sheet of printed cloth, really, that covers an arched entrance — parts, sending dozens of pigeons flying in all directions, and a tall gentleman appears. He is a nawab, a nobleman of ancient heritage, who, after many welcoming salaams, leads us into a vast chamber decked out with dusty chandeliers and whirring ceiling fans. We sit and talk with members of his large family as exquisite, home-made fruit drinks — sharbats — some flavoured with sweetly aromatic khas roots, others with the purple, sweet-and-sour juice of tiny falsa berries, are served in Venetian glasses. Tootak, morsels of delicate semolina pastry filled with spicy minced meat, are passed around on a silver tray to provoke and then satisfy the palate. The nawab's family is fast running out of money and can hardly sustain the style of life it was once used to. But unfailing courtesy and an almost overwhelming sense of hospitality are in its blood and will be with it until the last breath is drawn.

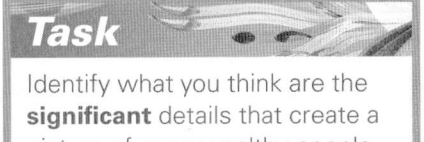

Task

Identify what you think are the **significant** details that create a picture of once-wealthy people who have fallen on hard times.

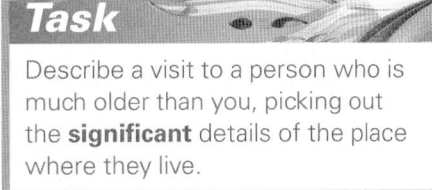

Task

Describe a visit to a person who is much older than you, picking out the **significant** details of the place where they live.

As the above extracts show, descriptive writing may be employed in all sorts of contexts. You might have to do some describing as part of a course-work task and most of the advice that follows applies equally well to this as to the examination.

Preparing to write

There is no simple set of rules for how to go about writing to describe but there are some general guidelines you should take into consideration.

A basic rule is that you **must not attempt to tell a story**. In other words, you are being asked to **observe**, not give an account. Think of description as an art exam in words: you have to paint a picture. For example, if you were asked to describe a shopping centre around Christmas time, you should think of the sights and sounds, the throngs of people, perhaps the expressions of desperation on their faces as they struggle with their mounds of last-minute shopping. If you chose instead to write about your day out at the shopping centre, it could work but the likelihood is that you would get bogged down with listing everything you did, with little real description.

Structure

Like any other piece of writing, your description needs a structure and shape. It should not simply be a list of features. Although you must not tell a story, a **simple** narrative structure may be appropriate, as in Extract 4 — the arrival in Jamaica. For the Christmas example, you could hang your description on a walk through the shopping centre or you could build your writing around different times of the day.

Focus and theme

You cannot write about everything — if you tried, your description would become cluttered with meaningless details. Give your writing a point and select the appropriate **significant details**. You could concentrate on the shoppers and their behaviour and link these with the idea of 'happy' Christmas. Or you could focus on all the glitter and what it suggests to you about the season.

Point of view

You will probably write as though you are the narrator, but there is no reason why you shouldn't put yourself in someone else's shoes if it helps to give a sharper picture. For instance, how about describing the shopping centre from the shop assistant's viewpoint or that of a security guard? This strategy may limit the range of aspects you deal with but can help you develop a structure and focus.

Task

Bearing these guidelines in mind, look closely at the picture and describe the scene in an interesting way.

Below is a list of points to think about. Don't answer the questions directly, but use them to explore ways of describing the scene and giving it a focus.

* Is it a landscape strange to British eyes?
* What sort of place is it?
* What meets the eye?
* Who are the children?
* Are they lost or is this where they live?
* What are they doing?
* Are they frightened or excited?
* What do the buildings suggest to you?
* Do you want to visit this place?
* Is it inviting or threatening?

Vocabulary

There is no magic formula for writing descriptions but there are a number of factors that should be considered when you are considering exactly how to write. The wider your vocabulary the better, but equally important are the **kinds** of words you choose and **how** you use them.

First, be **precise**. If you have returned from a holiday and someone asks what it was like, you might reply along the lines of, 'It was great. The weather was fantastic. It was sunny and hot every day and the beaches were huge.' That is fine in normal conversation but it doesn't do much for a reader because the vocabulary is weak and obvious.

Task

Replace the highlighted words with more interesting vocabulary. You may rewrite the sentences if you wish.

Using words to conjure up pictures in the reader's imagination is a difficult task because if you only name or itemise features, your writing is likely to be flat. As you think about what words to use, it is just as important to think about what they **suggest** as to consider what they mean literally.

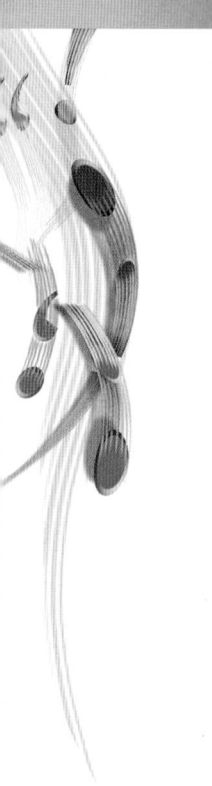

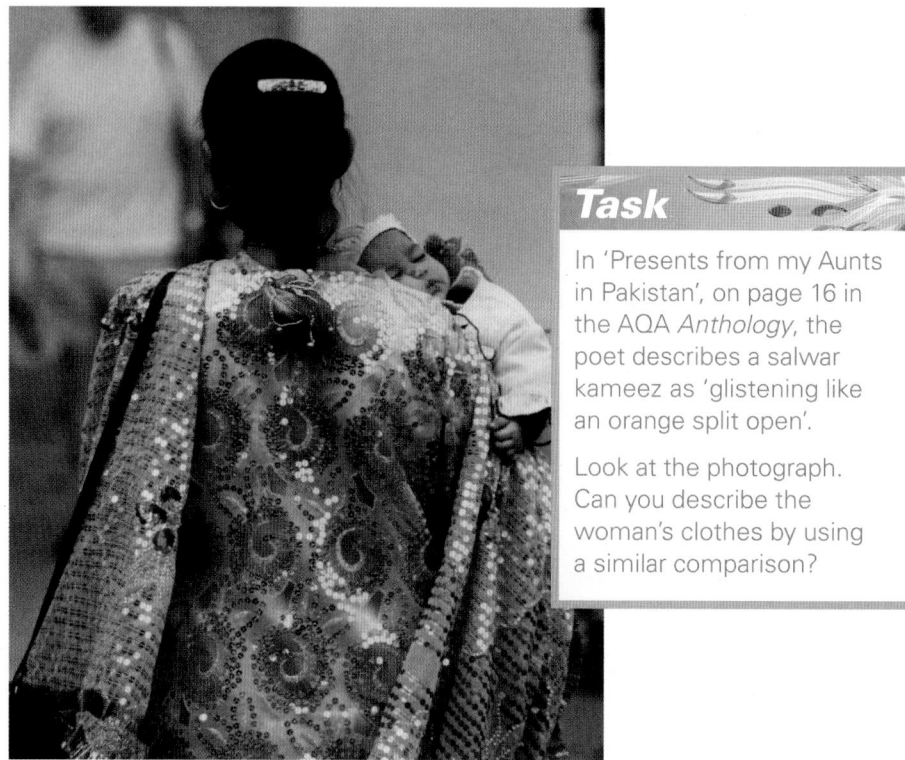

Task

In 'Presents from my Aunts in Pakistan', on page 16 in the AQA *Anthology*, the poet describes a salwar kameez as 'glistening like an orange split open'.

Look at the photograph. Can you describe the woman's clothes by using a similar comparison?

How you are assessed

For writing to inform and explain and writing to describe, as in all the other aspects of the English and English Literature examinations, you are assessed according to a mark scheme that reflects the Assessment Objectives. These are set out in Chapter 4.

In the case of writing to describe, the key element is how far the reader is able to see through the candidate's eyes, as it were. There should be a clear focus on the place or situation. Of course, all the other objectives concerning general writing skills apply too.

Task

Describe your ideal home.

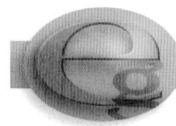 ### Examples of student performance

Student answer 1

My ideal home would be a massive mansion in the countryside surrounded by hundreds of miles of fields. When you go in there would be a massive hall with 60-inch plasma TVs on all the walls. The bedrooms would be huge with waterbeds and all the bathrooms would have pink jacuzzis. The garage would be full of my collection of Ferraris and I would race them around my private racetrack in the back garden.

In front of the house would be some beautiful flowerbeds designed by Charlie Dimmock. As I have my own rock band, there would be a massive studio in the basement with the best recording equipment and I would have 10,000-watt speakers in every room.

Examiner's comment

The candidate writes clear sentences, but they are all plain statements forming a list. The home is a fantasy house which is not imagined in any clear detail. The vague descriptive word 'massive' is overused; the list of objects is used as a substitute for describing, and the few descriptive adjectives ('huge', 'pink', 'beautiful', 'best') are weak in their effect. There are no paragraphs to separate the different aspects of the house. The answer would merit a Grade F.

Student answer 2

My ideal home would be a chateau, deep in rural France. The peace would be so relaxing and I would not feel a care in the world. I imagine approaching the mansion through a long line of trees. The sun glints on the fairy-tale turrets.

You would enter a spacious hall lined with portraits looking down on the visitor.

A sweeping staircase leads up to the first floor. Bedrooms lead off a long corridor. Although the house is very old, the bedrooms are luxurious and tastefully decorated. Needless to say, all have en-suite bathrooms, with stylish baths and showers. The latest technology is everywhere. Every living room has the latest hi-fi and wide-screen televisions and the kitchen is a chef's dream.

Examiner's comment

The candidate describes a fantasy house but it is defined as a chateau. There is a range of clear features, described with a conscious choice of vocabulary for descriptive effect: 'long line', 'sun glints', 'spacious', 'sweeping' etc. The sentence structures are varied and the use of paragraphs clearly separates different aspects of the house. Phrases such as 'needless to say' and 'chef's dream' create a tongue-in-cheek tone that prevents the description from being merely a list of luxuries. The candidate would receive a secure Grade C.

Student answer 3

Home is where you make it. It's easy to fantasise about living in a steel and glass dream, stuffed with every conceivable technological wonder and spending one's days sinking into jacuzzis or basking in never-ending summer.

For me home is where I am happy. It is a private place that I have made my own.

What bliss, to settle down for an evening comforted by the objects you love; the moth-eaten teddy bear, the mottled photograph of that school trip, the out-of-tune piano my grandmother left me, and my cat, Charlie, sinking his claws into my knee.

Where is it? Perhaps it is a romantic cottage nestling in the picturesque world of *Midsomer Murders*; perhaps it is a chaotic flat in the bustling community of Notting Hill; perhaps it is a ticky-tacky house in some labyrinthine housing estate, where happy families live in peaceful contentment, knowing that they are worth it.

Examiner's comment

This candidate focuses on the idea of a home rather than a house, a good example of thinking differently. He shows an awareness of what the obvious answer might be by satirising those who merely describe a dream house.

The candidate does not seem to describe much, but the picture of a contented evening is precisely captured by the careful selection of key details. Unusually, he employs a rhetorical flourish by characterising different places to live in terms of popular television and film. The use of cliché, such as 'romantic cottage', is deliberate. There is a consistent, controlled and effective use of vocabulary and sentence construction together with a strong personal style. The candidate would be awarded a Grade A.

English coursework

Media coursework

Although you obviously need to understand media texts (i.e. film, newspapers, adverts, television and so on) to complete this piece of work, you will actually be marked on the way you **write about** the texts.

The specification states that the media coursework assignment should be a 'substantial piece of written work which demonstrates the candidate's ability to respond to a text or texts through **analysis**, **review** and **comment**'.

✳ **Analysis**: this means looking at a text in depth and exploring how it works. You might analyse the typical characters found in a television sitcom or the types of plot found in a certain film genre.

✳ **Review**: literally, looking over something again. In the context of English/ English Literature, reviewing is connected to criticism. A good review involves analysis and comment, so these three points are actually closely linked.

✳ **Comment**: you are required to discuss how effective the media text is. For example, if you looked at magazine covers, you could comment on which ones grabbed your attention; if you were considering a film, you could comment on whether the filmmakers achieved what you think they set out to do.

Example: the horror film genre

The following sample task looks at the genre of horror films. Horror films are hugely popular. From the early silent horror films such as *Dracula* (1931) and *Frankenstein* (1931), audiences have lapped them up. Apparently we all like to be terrified and will pay good money to be scared witless.

Although there may seem to be many different types of horror film, they are all essentially reworkings of the same story. A major work of writing in this genre is Bram Stoker's novel *Dracula* (1897), which contains the elements found in all horror movies. A key point to note about the novel is its Gothic settings.

The Gothic period was actually from the twelfth to the sixteenth century and produced some of Europe's most famous cathedrals. When applied to literature or film, the term 'Gothic' means a story set among Gothic-type buildings. The genre is also connected with the supernatural, darkness, horror and terror. The key elements of the horror film genre are:

- There is a monster (though it might be unseen).
- There is a group of stupid individuals, usually some variation on a couple, who couldn't recognise a monster if it bit them on the head.
- The stupid people tend to go wandering about at night in draughty castles and big houses (no one does this in real life).
- The monster cannot be killed easily (handy for sequels).
- An expert always turns up with just the right type of ludicrous information about killing the monster.
- The minor characters are there to be killed — preferably one of these will be a pretty girl, but a dim boyfriend will do.
- There will be an unbelievable number of near misses with the monster before it is caught.
- Some mysticism from an exotic foreign land usually comes in useful for defeating the monster and the powers of darkness in general.
- The audience is given huge clues as to what is about to happen. The greatest clue is usually in the music.

To complete the tasks in this section you need to have watched a horror film. It is often more effective (and more enjoyable) to write about a film that was terrible — you can have fun tearing it to bits.

Dracula and Mina, wandering about in the dark woods in the 1931 film version of *Dracula*.

Task

Analyse and comment on the ways in which the directors of horror films use the elements listed below to create the following response in their audience:
* expectation   * fear   * sympathy

As part of your answer you should review at least one horror film.

Sample review: Dracula *(Tod Browning, 1931)*

Dracula concerns the young, ambitious Jonathan Harker who is sent to Transylvania to aid Count Dracula in purchasing property in England. When he gets to the castle he notices the following strange details:

* Dracula appears only at night.
* Dracula never seems to eat.
* There are no mirrors in the castle.
* Many rooms are locked to Harker.

This worries him a bit, but of course he hasn't the benefit of having seen loads of Dracula films, so he stays around. Dracula tells him to stay in certain parts of the castle for his own safety, so of course he goes wandering around in the parts that are off limits. When doing this he is nearly dined upon by three vampire women: Dracula saves him at the last moment. When Harker finally escapes from the castle, Dracula has set sail for England.

Back in Whitby, Harker's fiancée Mina and her friend Lucy are on holiday. They witness the arrival of a strange ship, blown impossibly into port during a freak storm. There is only one crew member aboard and he is dead and tied to the wheel. A large black dog is seen running up the steps to the ruined abbey. The ship's cargo is numerous large boxes.

Lucy starts to sleepwalk and appears pale each morning. It takes her friends ages to notice two puncture wounds in her neck and even then it requires the arrival of Professor Van Helsing to put the loss of blood together with the wounds. Her friends really are very dim.

Van Helsing is not in time to save her, despite tonnes of wild garlic and strategically placed crucifixes. She dies — apparently. Actually she is now a vampire, one of the undead. The men, including her fiancé, Arthur, witness her wandering about the churchyard in her nightie and decide to kill her. Luckily for all concerned, the professor has by now become an expert on vampires and how to kill them. He drives a stake through her heart and cuts off her head, which doesn't please Arthur too much.

The group of friends — Mina and Jonathan, Arthur, Van Helsing and two others — set about finding the boxes Dracula brought to England, as they now know, again very handily, that these contain earth from Transylvania which Dracula needs to sleep

on. They just happen to be living above a lunatic asylum (very Victorian) and one of the lunatics has invited Dracula in to see him. This means the count can now enter the house as he wishes (vampires can only enter a house if they have been invited).

Mina begins to look unwell, sleep badly and have terrible dreams. Do our friends see the similarities to Lucy? Of course not. They do not even notice the puncture wounds in her neck. She has now been infected and will turn into a vampire when she dies, unless Dracula is killed first. By now the men have found the boxes of earth, so Dracula has to make a run for it.

A chase ensues as the heroes race to head off Dracula before he can return to his castle. They nearly catch him, then actually catch him and kill him. Mina is saved, as is the rest of the civilised world. Lucky really.

Examiner's comment

Clearly this is not a full film review. There is no mention of the cast, the direction or the level of success the filmmakers achieved.

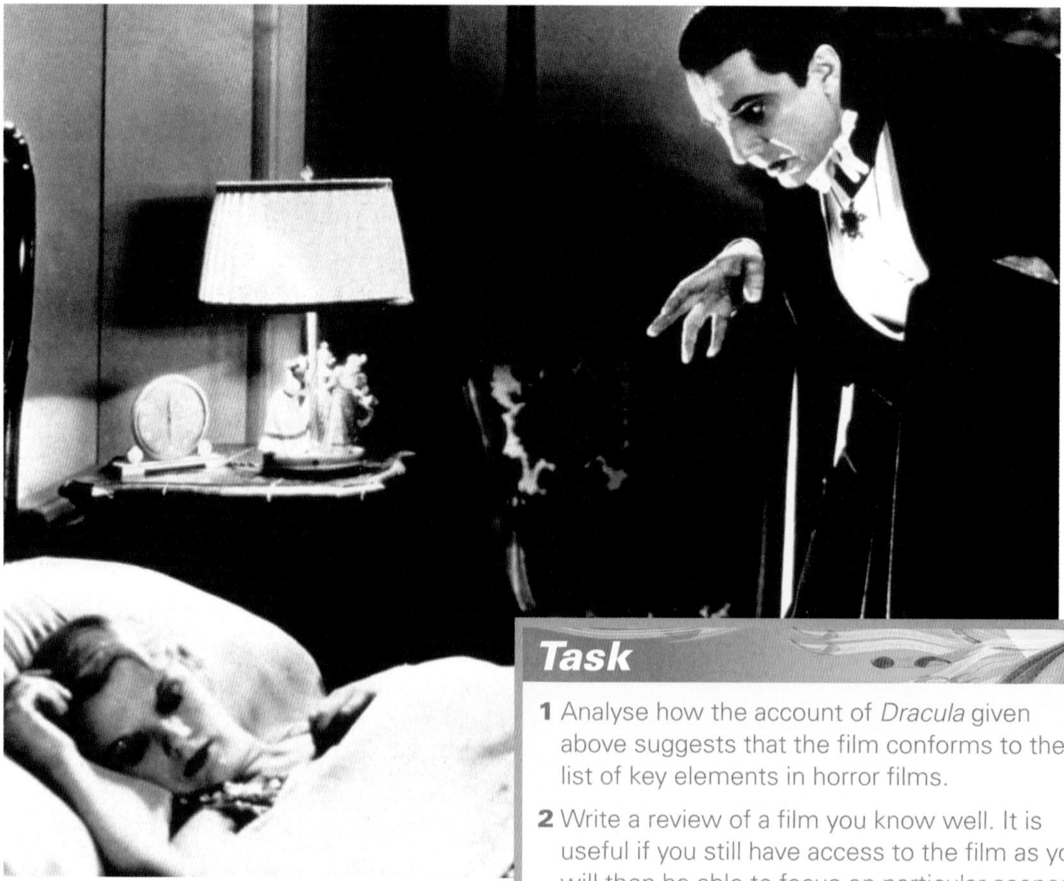

Task

1 Analyse how the account of *Dracula* given above suggests that the film conforms to the list of key elements in horror films.

2 Write a review of a film you know well. It is useful if you still have access to the film as you will then be able to focus on particular scenes.

Sample opening to a review

The Mummy (Terence Fisher, 1959) and its sequels follow the same pattern. Archaeologists bring a mummy back to England, it wakes up and goes on the rampage. The scientists try to work out what is happening and some Egyptian mystics confuse everyone, including themselves.

Hammer/Kobal

The chase sequences are classically funny. The Mummy walks very slowly yet always manages to catch its victims who, in reality, would have escaped with a nifty side-step. This brings to light one more 'fact' about horror films, which is that no matter how quickly the pursued character runs, the monster always overtakes.

Examiner's comment

The tone of this review is partly the result of viewing an old film through modern eyes. There is always a place for comment on the way the original audience would probably have received a film.

Task

Having watched a horror film, complete the following preparation for writing a detailed review.

1 List the main characters and say which category each fits into, e.g. scientist, idiot victim, pretty girl who is nearly killed etc.

2 Compare your list with the next horror film you see. You will probably be able to come up with the same categories.

3 Note the setting of each film. Is it Gothic?

4 Comment on the music, e.g. high-pitched violins, low timpani drums.

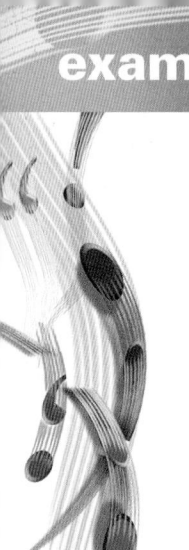

> ### Task
>
> Write a **review** of a horror film you have watched. **Analyse** how the film obeys the conventions of the horror genre and comment on how effective you thought the film was.

Original writing coursework

This section continues with the example of the horror genre. By now you should have looked at the typical elements that make up a piece of horror writing. You might have watched one or two horror films in your study. To prepare this piece of coursework, you will use all you have learned about the horror film genre.

Use media resources on the horror genre to complete the following tasks.

> ### Task
>
> Write the outline of a spoof horror film. Your piece of writing should be approximately 1,000 words long.
>
> You could take the following approaches to the assignment:
>
> **a** Use the plot of an existing horror film and deliberately exaggerate the various elements, e.g. have a big sign outside Dracula's castle that reads 'Vampire abode — entrance fee one pint' to make it even more obvious that no one would ever spend the night there.
>
> **b** Base your idea around a monster so unscary as to be ridiculous.
>
> **c** Bring together many obvious horror film elements, e.g. a honeymoon couple whose car breaks down in Transylvania under a full moon on Friday the thirteenth.
>
> **d** Create a series of situations which usually lead to trouble for all concerned in a horror film, such as exploring an old house at night or walking through a park even though there is a crazed killer on the loose. You could set this up repeatedly but have your stupid central character emerge safely each time.

> ### Task
>
> Write a series of diary entries about your visit to a typical horror film location, e.g. Transylvania.
>
> You could include any of the following features:
>
> **a** Deliberately exaggerate the setting, e.g. a creepy castle up a mountain, lit by candles and occasional flashes of lightning.

Task *(continued)*

b Fill the location with obvious horror film stereotypes such as the scary butler or the mad scientist.

c Always visit the attic and the cellar, preferably at night.

d Ignore all warnings from strange village folk about bad things up at the castle.

e Be involved in a ridiculous series of near misses with various horror genre monsters.

English Literature
Section A

Post-1914 prose

Section A of the English Literature examination paper requires you to answer one question on post-1914 prose texts. There are two options: *either* one of the novels prescribed by AQA *or* two of the short stories from the AQA *Anthology*.

Assessment Objectives

The overall skills you must demonstrate in your answers on post-1914 prose are set out in the Assessment Objectives for English Literature. You must demonstrate your ability to:

AO1	Respond to texts critically, sensitively and in detail, selecting suitable ways to convey your response, using textual evidence as appropriate.
AO2	Explore how language, structure and forms contribute to the meaning of texts, considering different approaches to texts and alternative interpretations.
AO3	Explore relationships and comparisons within and between texts, selecting and evaluating relevant material.

Know your texts

In practice, whatever the Assessment Objective, you must **know your texts in detail**. Many students rely on the fact that they can take their texts into the examination and look up suitable passages and quotations on the spot. But there is no substitute for reading and preparing your texts beforehand, so that in the examination you know exactly **what** you want to find and exactly **where** to find it.

Remember, you cannot take notes of any kind into the examination. Although you can consult your texts in the exam, they must not contain annotations. This means you must know your way around the texts well. Novels, in particular, are bulky and it is often difficult to find a precise quotation quickly.

In the case of a novel or short story you must first know the sequence of events. The plot can be mapped out using a diagram or timeline. It takes practice, but designing a diagram that sets out the main plot, any sub-plot, where new characters are introduced and so on really enables you to get to grips with the text. The opening of the plot of *To Kill a Mockingbird* is given in the diagram below.

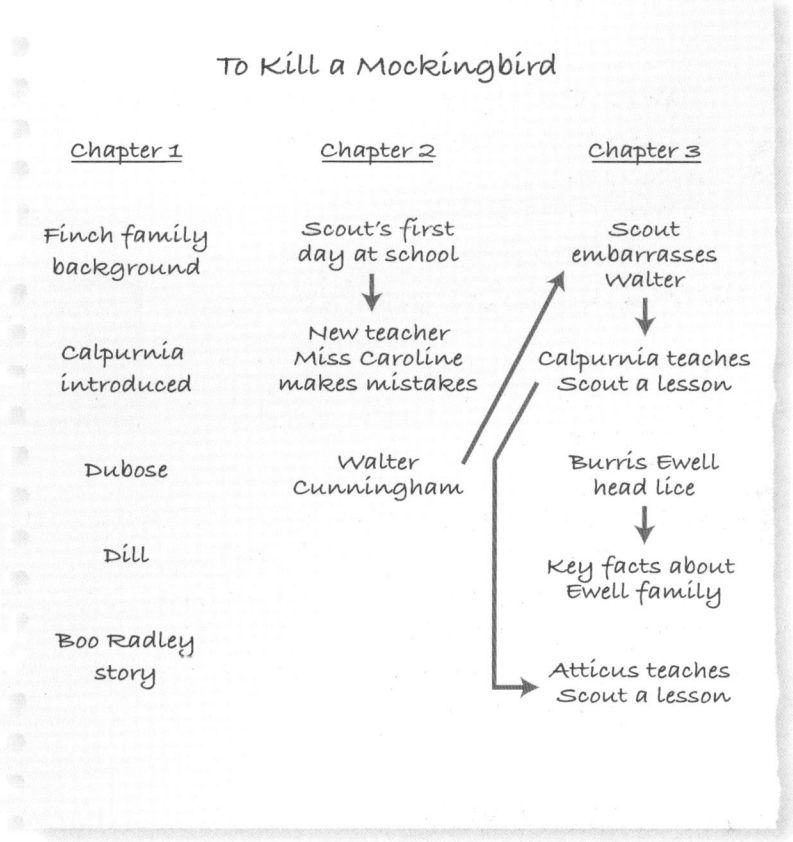

Although you will not be able to take it into the examination with you, it is a good idea to keep a quotation book, which you can use as a reminder of the detailed features of your text(s) when you are revising. A useful way of setting it out is to write appropriate quotations on one page and a suitable comment on the other. For instance, an entry on Leslie Norris's 'Snowdrops' might look like this:

'He tried to think what they would look like'	Childhood imagination/innocence — readiness to wonder
'"That's nice," said his mother'	Adult indifference to magical world of young/abrupt statement/too busy with everyday matters
'His mother coughed and looked sharply at the boy'	Wants to protect boy from adult world

The advantage of keeping a notebook in this way is that it helps you get to know the text(s) from two angles:

❉ You can read through the quotations and think about what you would use them for.

❉ You can read through the comments and think about what quotations you could use to illustrate your points.

You can add to your quotations and comments as you begin to understand the texts better, but it is a good idea to keep your notes as clear as possible and not too lengthy.

> **Note:** you will find a quotation book especially useful for last-minute revision when you don't have time to reread a whole novel.

Commenting

The AOs can be satisfied only through **commenting** on the text(s). This can be defined as saying something about a text that **isn't already stated directly**.

Look at the opening of 'Snowdrops'. It does not matter if you are not studying this particular story because the same principles apply to the close reading of any text.

Today Miss Webster was going to show them the snowdrops growing in the little three-cornered garden outside the school-keeper's house, where they weren't allowed to go. All through the winter, Miss Webster said, the snowdrops had been asleep under the ground, but now they were up, growing in the garden. He tried to think what they would look like, but all he could imagine was one flake of the falling snow, bitterly frail and white, and nothing like a flower.

It was a very cold morning. He leaned against the kitchen table, feeling the hard edge against his chest, eating his breakfast slowly. His brother, Geraint, who was only three, sat in an armchair close to the fire. He could see the shape of Geraint's

head outlined against the flames and he saw with wonder that the fire had given to his brother's legs a glow of red only slightly less bright than the leaping flames. Geraint was eating a bowl of porridge, and what he did was this. He would make a crater in the porridge with his spoon, and then he'd watch the milk run in and fill the hole up. Then he would dip his spoon in the milk and drink it. The boy watched his brother.

'Hurry up,' said the boy's mother, 'or you'll never get to school!'

'Miss Webster is going to show us the snowdrops today,' he said.

'That's nice,' said his mother, looking out of the window at the grey morning. 'I wonder where your father is.'

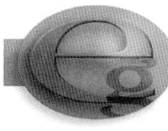

Examples of student performance

Here are three student responses that explain what the opening of the short story shows us about the character of the young boy.

Student answer 1

At the beginning of the story the boy thinks about the snowdrops, which his teacher has promised to show his class. He is very excited because he has never seen snowdrops before: 'He tried to think what they would look like, but all he could imagine was one flake of the falling snow, bitterly frail and white, and nothing like a flower.'

When he has his breakfast, he notices how red his brother's legs have become from sitting in front of the fire. When he tells his mother about the snowdrops, all she says is, 'That's nice.' This is an abrupt statement.

Examiner's comment

The candidate is familiar with aspects of the text and is able to identify appropriate features that relate to the child's experience. There is some response to the boy's feelings about the snowdrops ('He is very excited'); although there is a simple identification of an effect ('abrupt statement'), the candidate has probably learned this phrase and does not know what it means. This response would receive a Grade F.

Student answer 2

The boy is excited about the prospect of seeing the snowdrops and his imagination is stirred as he wonders about these mysterious flowers which he has never seen before: 'He tried to think what they would look like, but all he could imagine was one flake of the falling snow, bitterly frail and white, and nothing like a flower.'

As he sits eating his breakfast he still appears to be dreaming as he marvels at the glowing legs of his brother, sitting before the fire. However, we feel he must be disappointed by his mother's abrupt, uninterested reply, when he tells her about the snowdrops.

Examiner's comment

The candidate comments on the boy's excitement and links it to the world of his imagination, a point supported by the selection of the detail concerning his brother. He is able to come to wider conclusions based on the text ('he still appears to be dreaming'). Both the mother's tone of voice and its possible effect on the child ('he must be disappointed') are recognised.

The first answer consists mainly of statements that are not much more than a retelling of the story. The two single words 'excited' and 'abrupt', which amount to simple **comment**, are worth as much as the rest of the answer combined. The second answer is much better because the candidate has tried to concentrate on the boy's feelings first and to show how we find out about them from examining details in the text for clues. The candidate would gain a Grade C.

Student answer 3

Leslie Norris's story explores the way in which the world of childhood innocence and wonder meets the harsher world of adult experience. The opening paragraphs already provide hints of what is to come.

For the child, the snowdrops are a source of mystery and wonder. As he thinks of what they are called, he can only imagine them as magical as a snowflake, 'bitterly frail and white'. Although we do not recognise it at the time, these words are prophetic and look forward to the poignant conclusion of the story, as Miss Webster trembles like a snowdrop at the passing of the funeral procession of her dead lover.

The power of the childhood imagination is further emphasised as the child observes 'with wonder' his brother's legs glowing from the red of the fire, and even his porridge becomes a miniature landscape seen through a child's eye. However, the first hint of a different sort of experience breaks in when the mother responds abruptly and without any understanding of the child's announcement that Miss Webster is to show her class the snowdrops.

Examiner's comment

The candidate has a secure grasp of the different levels of meaning in the story. There is no attempt to list what happens, but rather a clear understanding that the author, who is mentioned by name, has a purpose and design. The candidate appreciates that even the simple details of the opening have a significance that will not be grasped fully until later.

The candidate begins by establishing one of the story's underlying themes and then uses the details of the text to illustrate this. She gives brief, **precise quotation**, and where there is no quotation there is clear **reference**. Notice that student answer 1 only tells you **what happens** but student answer 3 makes continuous **comment**. This answer would receive a Grade A.

> **Task**
>
> You may or may not know 'Snowdrops', but look at the opening section and the three answers above and write as much as you can on what you have learned about the story.

> **Task**
>
> Start a quotation notebook on your set novel or stories with the quotations on one side and the comments on the other. If you are studying 'Snowdrops', you need to add to the notes already provided on page 158.

We have seen that telling the story is not the same as commenting on a text, so what should you write about in order to comment? The answer will vary a little from text to text and depend to an extent on the question you are asked, but there are some features that are common to most prose texts.

Plot

The storyline or plot is the most obvious feature of any story. The reader's basic interest is in what happens next and writers construct their plots around the desire to know.

Beginnings and endings are particularly important. Think about how they connect, or how the ending draws the strands of the story together and perhaps even makes sense of the story.

You need to think about **how** the plot works. A plot is often like a game between the author and the reader. The author may give you pieces of information to start you guessing and lead you on, but you may not know the whole truth until the end of the story. The plot may be constructed so as to create suspense or to contain unexpected connections or coincidences.

Character

Most stories involve at least one character. Some characters may be more important than others. You need to consider what characters are like and the part they play in the whole story. Sometimes a character may be the centre of interest; at other times the characters may represent an aspect of human feeling and behaviour, such as consideration for others or a lust for power.

Remember that characters in novels and short stories are not real people. They are created by the writer for a purpose, which is often to do with the theme.

Theme

Authors mainly write stories to make a point about experience and life. The point may be about concerns like injustice or racism, or matters such as love or growing up. The central concerns of a story are its themes. Writers do not

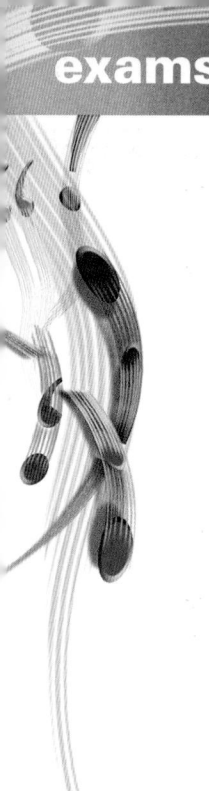

often tell you what their themes are; it is up to the reader to appreciate the writer's concerns. Stories and novels often have more than one theme.

The ability to understand and demonstrate knowledge of the themes of a text is valued highly by examiners.

Dialogue

Novels and stories often contain dialogue, which generally serves a purpose. We can learn a great deal from the dialogue in a text. In real life it is obvious when a person is being sarcastic, is after something or is overcome with emotion. In the same way, you can usually detect what characters in novels and stories are feeling. Think about how characters relate to others and watch out for the way a character reacts to something that is said to him/her. Students are often good at writing about what characters say but forget that analysing characters' reactions to what is said is just as important.

Remember when you read dialogue that the characters are talking to each other as well as to the audience, and that they are in a situation or context. When you talk to another person you have to interpret what is said to you as well as think about what you are saying. If, for example, you want to borrow some money, you are unlikely to just say 'Lend me £20'. You might ask, 'Could you lend me some money?' and then wait for a reaction before going further. Or you might be more subtle and say, 'Would you do me a favour?' Think about how you would answer that — it would be difficult to say 'No'.

Although you are not asked to write about a play in the examination, plays are helpful examples when thinking about dialogue as they consist almost entirely of speech and rely on the ways characters interact. Here is a short extract from the opening of a play by Harold Pinter entitled *Trouble in the Works* (1961). The setting is Mr Fibbs's office. Mr Wills knocks at the door and enters.

Fibbs: Ah, Wills. Good. Come in. Sit down, will you?
Wills: Thanks Mr Fibbs.
Fibbs: You got my message?
Wills: I just got it.
Fibbs: Good. Good.

At first you might think nothing much has happened, but if you look again there is evidence of the relationship between the two men in the way they address each other: *Mr* Fibbs is the employer, and he calls his employee Wills. This is also revealed by the context; Mr Wills is given permission to come in and he waits to be asked to sit down.

But the short sentences and repetition suggest that it is the employer who is nervous. He also states the obvious; if Mr Wills had not got his message he would not be in the office. The conversation then continues after a pause. Why do you think Mr Fibbs pauses? Is he thinking about what to say next? Is he about to raise a difficult subject? Is this more evidence that he is nervous?

Fibbs: Good. Well now… Have a cigar?
Wills: No thanks, not for me, Mr Fibbs.
Fibbs: Well now Wills, I hear there's been a little trouble in the factory?
Wills: Yes, I…I suppose you could call it that.

Why does Fibbs make the offer of a cigar? Could he be putting off what he has to say? Is he trying to make a friendly gesture so that Wills will listen sympathetically? Note that Fibbs continues to repeat words. When he gets to the point, he describes it as 'a little trouble' — why? Do you think Wills really agrees with this description?

Language

Writers use detailed language to create effects or to emphasise aspects of the story and its themes. The important skill is to show how a particular word or phrase relates to the bigger picture. (See Chapter 2.)

Setting

Whether or not a particular scene or setting is important will depend on the story. Often the setting will establish a context: if it is a crowded neighbourhood, where everyone knows everyone, the reader may form a different picture from if the setting were a remote country district.

Point of view

Stories may be told from the point of view of a first-person narrator, from that of a character in the story (i.e. the third person), or from the point of view of an observer, who could be the author or a character. There are many different approaches.

Mood

Mood is the overall feeling of a story or part of a story, such as sadness, light-heartedness, tension, joy etc. For instance, the conclusion of Doris Lessing's 'Flight' (AQA *Anthology*, pages 59–62) could be described as bittersweet or both sad and happy. On the one hand, the girl empathises with the old man and the pain he must feel because she is no longer his little girl. On the other hand, the old man can still look on his granddaughter with a sense of pride.

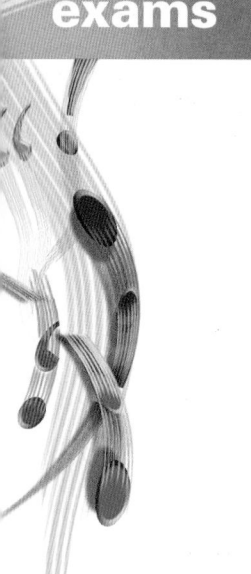

Remember that some or all of the above features will figure in any story, but you should try to focus on what is most important. For example, the stories in the *Anthology* focus on childhood or a learning experience. It is better to concentrate first on a **theme** and then explore how features such as setting and dialogue bring out the ideas.

> ## Task
>
> Look again at the extract from 'Snowdrops' on pages 158–159. Write **eight** sentences, each one making a comment on one of the topics discussed above (plot, character, theme, dialogue, language, setting, point of view, mood).

If you have worked through the tasks that have been set so far, you may feel that you have been repeating yourself. That is exactly the point: it is only through looking at your texts as many times as possible, in as many ways as possible, that you can be in control.

Linking and comparing

So far we have considered the set texts in the light of Assessment Objective 1 (responding critically and in detail) and Assessment Objective 2 (exploring language and structure). To gain a Grade C or above you must also consider Assessment Objective 3, which involves **making comparisons and finding links**.

❊ If you are studying the short stories you must be able to compare or contrast them in some way.

❊ If you are studying a single novel you should be able to see connections between parts of the text, although you will probably not be asked to make any direct comparisons.

To make comparisons and find links you must prepare well; it would be an impossible task to do entirely in the exam.

Short stories

In the exam, read the question carefully and consider what it is you are being asked to compare. It might ask for a comparison of how any of the features listed above play a part in two stories (i.e. plot, character, theme, dialogue, language, setting, point of view, mood).

> **Note** that the word 'compare' will appear in the question.

Be alert to the **wording** of the question. For example, you may have lots of notes on individual characters but the question refers to 'relationships'. You would therefore need to **adapt your ideas** so that you focus on how the characters behave towards one another. You would not have to put together a completely fresh set of ideas. Similarly, a question asking you about beginnings or endings is about a particular aspect of plotting — do not write everything you know about the whole plot.

Novels

Exam questions do not usually ask you to make comparisons between particular sections of the novel, but you are often directed to part of the text and asked to explain its significance. Alternatively, you may be asked about a general aspect of the novel, such as the depiction of children.

You will always gain extra credit if you can demonstrate that there are **connections** between different parts of the novel. At the very least, draw your evidence from a **variety of places** in the book. For example, a central character in *To Kill a Mockingbird* is Atticus, who appears to be a firm but gentle, bookish father. A key scene in the novel is when, to many people's amazement, he shoots a rabid dog; he is a crack shot but never normally picks up a gun. Even if you haven't read the novel, you should be able to understand how that action was a revelation to his children, who regarded their father as a bit of a fuddy-duddy. There is plenty to write about the dog-shooting scene alone, but a candidate who links it to other scenes in the novel, to throw light on the character, would gain many more marks.

Read the short story below. It is not one of the set texts for the examination but it is amusing and you may enjoy reading it. At first it may seem that the story is entirely silly, but consider the title. It is called 'A Fable', which suggests it has a moral.

The young man was clean shaven and neatly dressed. It was early Monday morning and he got on the subway. It was the first day of his first job and he was slightly nervous; he didn't know exactly what his job would be. Otherwise he felt fine. He loved everybody he saw. He loved everybody on the street and everybody disappearing into the subway, and he loved the world because it was a fine clear day and he was starting his first job.

Without kicking anybody, the young man was able to find a seat on the Manhattan-bound train. The car filled quickly and he looked up at the people standing over him envying his seat. Among them were a mother and daughter who were going shopping. The daughter was a beautiful girl with blond hair and soft-looking skin, and he was immediately attracted to her.

'He's staring at you,' the mother whispered to the daughter.

'Yes, Mother, I feel so uncomfortable. What shall I do?'

'He's in love with you.'

'In love with me? How can you tell?'

'Because I'm your mother.'

'But what shall I do?'

'Nothing. He'll try to talk to you. If he does, answer him. Be nice to him. He's only a boy.'

The train reached the business district and many people got off. The girl and her mother found seats opposite the young man. He continued to look at the girl who occasionally looked to see if he was looking at her.

The young man found a good pretext for standing in giving his seat to an elderly man. He stood over the girl and her mother. They whispered back and forth and looked up at him. At another stop the seat next to the girl was vacated, and the young man blushed but quickly took it.

'I knew it,' the mother said between her teeth. 'I knew it, I knew it.'

The young man cleared his throat and tapped the girl. She jumped.

'Pardon me,' he said. 'You're a very pretty girl.'

'Thank you,' she said.

'Don't talk to him,' her mother said. 'Don't answer him. I'm warning you. Believe me.'

'I'm in love with you,' he said to the girl.

'I don't believe you,' the girl said.

'Don't answer him,' the mother said.

'I really do,' he said. 'In fact, I'm so much in love with you that I want to marry you.'

'Do you have a job?' she said.

'Yes, today is my first day. I'm going to Manhattan to start my first day of work.'

'What kind of work will you do?' she asked.

'I don't know exactly,' he said. 'You see, I didn't start yet.'

'It sounds exciting,' she said.

'It's my first job, but I'll have my own desk and handle a lot of papers and carry them around in a briefcase, and it will pay well, and I'll work my way up.'

'I love you,' she said.

'Will you marry me?'

'I don't know. You'll have to ask my mother.' The young man rose from his seat and stood before the girl's mother. He cleared his throat very carefully for a long time. 'May I have the honor of having your daughter's hand in marriage?' he said, but he was drowned out by the subway noise.

The mother looked up at him and said, 'What?' He couldn't hear her either, but he could tell by the movement of her lips and by the way her face wrinkled up that she said, What. The train pulled to a stop.

'May I have the honor of having your daughter's hand in marriage!' he shouted, not realizing there was no subway noise.

Everybody on the train looked at him, smiled, and then they all applauded.

'Are you crazy?' the mother asked. The train started again.

10

'What?' he said.

'Why do you want to marry her?' she asked.

'Well, she's pretty — I mean, — I'm in love with her.'

'Is that all?'

'I guess so,' he said. 'Is there supposed to be more?'

'No. Not usually,' the mother said. 'Are you working?'

'Yes. As a matter of fact, that's why I'm going into Manhattan so early. Today is the first day of my first job.'

'Congratulations,' the mother said.

'Thanks,' he said. 'Can I marry your daughter?'

'Do you have a car?' she asked.

'Not yet,' he said. 'But I should be able to get one pretty soon. And a house, too.'

'A house?'

'With lots of rooms.'

'Yes, that's what I expected you to say,' she said. She turned to her daughter. 'Do you love him?'

'Yes, Mother, I do.'

'Why?'

'Because he's good, and gentle, and kind.'

'Are you sure?'

'Yes.'

'Then you really love him.'

'Yes.'

'Are you sure there isn't anyone else that you might love and might want to marry?'

'No, Mother,' the girl said.

'Well, then,' the mother said to the young man. 'Looks like there's nothing I can do about it. Ask her again.'

The train stopped.

'My dearest one,' he said, 'will you marry me?'

'Yes,' she said.

Everybody in the car smiled and applauded.

'Isn't life wonderful?' the boy asked the mother.

'Beautiful,' the mother said.

The conductor climbed down from between the cars as the train started up and, straightening his dark tie, approached them with a solemn black book in his hand.

Robert Fox, 'A Fable', 1986

Task

Write a paragraph on what you think the story is trying to say about human relationships.

English Literature
Section B

Pre- and post-1914 poetry

Writing about poetry in the English Literature examination requires the same skills needed for writing on poetry from different cultures. Chapter 7 of this book contains detailed advice on how to write about poetry. The extra requirement for poetry in the literature examination is that you write about four poems — two from the post-1914 pair of poets that you have studied and two from the pre-1914 poetry bank.

Copy out the table below and fill in the pre-1914 boxes and poems for your set pair with the help of your teacher. Different classes might study different poems, and you need to be completely clear which ones you are studying.

> **Do not** decide in the exam that you fancy writing about a poem you have not read before.

	Pair 1	Poems	Pair 2	Poems
Your two set post-1914 poets	Seamus Heaney Gillian Clarke		Carol Ann Duffy Simon Armitage	
	Poems for comparison			
Poems from the 'Pre-1914 Poetry Bank' section of the AQA *Anthology*				

Comparing poems

No matter which tier of the examination paper you sit, you will be asked to compare poems. This means that you will not be writing about one poem on its own but will be making **links** between poems. As for the poems from different cultures, it is a good idea to look at how poems might be grouped together well before the examination.

Copy out the table below and write down the poems you are studying by the two set post-1914 poets.

Post-1914 poet	Poem title	Theme(s)

Now repeat the table for the pre-1914 poems you are studying. You can add them to the table as you come to them.

Keeping tables such as these in a notebook you use only for English is a useful way to organise your thoughts as you are learning. It is also invaluable when you come to revise. It could be the same notebook you use to keep quotations when preparing to write about your set prose text (see pages 157–158).

Assessment Objectives

The suggestion on the examination paper is that you spend 1 hour on the poetry question you choose to answer. This means that the most time you will spend on a single poem is about 10 minutes. (You need time to read and analyse the question and then to prepare your answer. You will also spend some time writing about the links between poems.) You therefore need to go into the exam knowing what you can usefully say in those 10 minutes. Focusing on the AOs will help you do this.

Remind yourself of the general guidelines:

Grade A	Explores meaning, purpose and language and evaluates effects on reader — detailed analysis of poems.
Grade C/D	Begins to understand the central ideas in the poem and grasp emotions — appropriate comment on meanings.
Grade F/G	Selects simple actions and writes about the storyline of the poem.

Your writing about poetry in the examination will be assessed against the same AOs as for writing about prose in English Literature:

AO1	Respond to texts critically, sensitively and in detail, using textual evidence as appropriate.
AO2	Explore how language, structure and forms contribute to the meaning of texts, considering different approaches to texts and alternative interpretations.
AO3	Explore relationships and comparisons within and between texts, selecting and evaluating relevant material.

AO1

Respond to texts critically, sensitively and in detail, using textual evidence as appropriate

Key words	What the key words mean
respond to texts critically	You are able to look beyond the storyline of the poem and can see that the poet has intended to make the reader think about a subject. You can make critical comments about whether or not the poet has been successful (not simply saying whether or not you like the poem).
respond to texts sensitively and in detail	You are able to see that the poems contain different ideas and can discuss elements such as mood and atmosphere. You can focus on a small detail of a poem if this is important in exploring the poet's ideas.
using textual evidence as appropriate	You can quote from the poem in the correct place to support your comments.

Task

Choose one of the poems from your pair of post-1914 poets and do the following:

❉ Discuss what ideas you think the poet was trying to get across.

❉ Say whether you think the poet was successful.

❉ Remember to support your comments with references to the poem.

AO2

Explore how language, structure and forms contribute to the meaning of texts, considering different approaches to texts and alternative interpretations

Key words	What the key words mean
explore how language contributes to the meaning of texts	You are able to look at the poet's language and see that words have been chosen for effect. You can see that the way a poem is written is not the only way it could have been written.
explore how structure and forms contribute to the meaning of texts	You can recognise the structure of a poem, e.g. use of stanzas, unusual layout. You know that certain poetic forms tend to be used for particular types of poetry and recognise that the form of a poem is an important part of its purpose, e.g. sonnets are often used for love poetry.
considering different approaches to texts and alternative interpretations	You recognise that poems can contain more than one possible meaning and that there are different interpretations depending on the reader.

Task

Choose one of the poems you have studied from the pre-1914 poetry bank.

Discuss the language features that appeal to you in this poem. Remember to:
❋ comment on the way the poet has used language
❋ say why these language features appeal to you

AO3

Explore relationships and comparisons within and between texts, selecting and evaluating relevant material

Key words	What the key words mean
explore relationships within and between texts	You can see how ideas relate to each other within any one poem. You can see how ideas can be linked across more than one poem; for example, this might mean considering how family life is discussed in more than one poem or looking at the ways in which different poems contain ideas about life and death.
explore comparisons within and between texts	You can compare ideas within one poem and recognise that there might be contrasts. You are able to compare and contrast different poems; for example, this could mean discussing how one poem sees nature as a kind force whereas another poem sees nature as dangerous and destructive.

Key words	What the key words mean
selecting and evaluating relevant material	You can select relevant parts of individual poems instead of simply making general comments on poems as a whole.

Task

Choose one poem by each of your pair of post-1914 poets and discuss the methods the poets use to present nature.

Remember to compare:
* the writers' attitudes to nature
* how the poets present nature by writing about it in different ways

Task

1 Compare how attitudes to family members are shown in one poem by each of your pair of post-1914 poets.

2 Compare how the attitudes of parents to their children are shown in two pre-1914 poems.

Task

Compare how emotions are explored in two pre-1914 poems and any two of the poems by your chosen pair of post-1914 poets.

Exam practice

In the exam you will be asked to compare across both sets of poems, i.e. the pre-1914 poems and the post-1914 poems. For example, you might have to:
* select one poem from each of the post-1914 poets, then compare these two poems with two pre-1914 poems
* compare one post-1914 poem and one pre-1914 poem on a given theme (such as childhood), then compare one more post-1914 poem with another pre-1914 poem on a different theme

This is actually more complicated to write down than it is to do. Remember, it is essential that you cross-reference between poems — simply writing about four poems in turn is not enough for you to progress beyond Grade D.

Doing well in Section B of the English Literature examination depends on organisation. The tables you were asked to complete at the start of this chapter should be useful as you begin to think about how to put together an answer based on four different poems.

Work through the following tasks, which all involve organising the poems into groups. Only attempt those that deal with the post-1914 poets you are studying.

Task

1 Select one poem by Heaney and one poem by Clarke that deal with difficult human relationships. Select two suitable poems from the pre-1914 poetry bank that could be compared with these poems.

2 Select one poem by Duffy and one poem by Armitage that deal with the subject of human relationships. Select two suitable poems from the pre-1914 poetry bank that could be compared with these poems.

3 Choose two pre-1914 poems that discuss the way mankind interacts with nature. Select one poem from each of your chosen post-1914 poets that could be compared with these poems.

4 Now repeat questions 1–3 for each of the following themes:
* childhood * danger * death
* anger * love * getting older

You can form your own questions by adapting the following general question to each of the themes listed above.

Task

Choose two pre-1914 poems that discuss [*insert chosen theme here*].
Select one poem from each of your chosen post-1914 poets that could be compared with these poems.

This kind of practice will help you become so familiar with the poems that you will not be thrown by the questions on the exam paper. You will have a choice of three questions, so you should easily find one that suits the poems you are most comfortable writing about.

Glossary

Throughout the English and English Literature examinations you are required to appreciate and discuss how writers use language to create effects and influence readers. There are a number of terms that are helpful when discussing language and they are defined below.

These terms are a kind of shorthand that will save you from giving lengthy explanations every time a particular language feature appears. They allow you to be more precise in your comments on a writer's language. For example, rather than saying, 'The writer uses a lot of descriptive language', you might say, 'The writer uses a large number of adjectives connected with colour'. However, simply knowing the terms does not necessarily indicate that you understand the language being used, any more than being able to identify a goalkeeper shows you really understand the game of football. In other words, you must be able to explain the effects they are creating. The entries also include some examination and media terms.

Active and passive verbs

We most often use verbs in the **active voice**:

> The dog **bit** the man.

We can turn this sentence into the **passive voice** quite simply:

> The man **was bitten** by the dog.

The passive form is generally regarded as more formal than the active. An important feature of the passive is that it can be *impersonal*, in the sense that it is not necessary to indicate who has performed an action. Watch out for media texts in which the passive is used to conceal the full facts. For example:

> Active: The company sacked its staff. (The company is responsible)
> Passive: The staff were sacked. (Who is responsible?)

Adjectives

Words such as 'green', 'exciting', 'happy', 'doubtful', 'extended' and 'difficult' are adjectives. Either they come before a noun and add to its sense, as in 'the happy children', or they can be connected with a noun through the verb '**to be**': 'The children were happy'.

The thoughtful use of adjectives can turn a vague statement into something richer and more precise.

Adverbs

Adverbs add information to verbs ('He ran **quickly**') and adjectives ('The music was **unbearably** loud').

Many adjectives can be turned into an adverb by the addition of '**–ly**': sad – sadly; strong – strongly; disappointing – disappointingly; furious – furiously. This is not a universal rule, however; you cannot say 'daftly' or 'greenly'.

Do not overuse adverbs in your writing, even if you can use them accurately. Used sparingly and for effect they can make your writing more sophisticated.

Alliteration

The technique of repeating the initial letter or sound in adjacent words to create an atmospheric or onomatopoeic effect, e.g. 'Degged with dew, dappled with dew'. Alliteration can also link words in the reader's mind to emphasise certain aspects of the sense.

Notice that alliteration is only to do with the sounds. It may draw attention to particular words, but you must be careful not to make exaggerated claims for alliteration, e.g. 'The poet uses alliteration to show he is angry'.

Analysis

Examining texts in detail, passing comment on features such as their construction, the author's methods, the feelings conveyed etc.

Argument

The organisation of information into a clear order that leads towards a conclusion.

Audience

The type of person, or people, you may be writing for.

Connotation

The connotations of a word are its associations or overtones. They can be as important as its primary meaning. It is often useful to group the connotations of words in a poem, for example, into **positive**, **negative** and **neutral**

associations. The 'weighting' of the words can reveal a lot about the overall mood of the text.

Dialect

Dialect is a way of speaking usually associated with a region or country. Writers often use dialect forms to lend authenticity to their work. West Indian writers, in particular, use dialect forms to make their work a true reflection of their culture (e.g. in 'Half-Caste').

Remember that dialect is not incorrect English. It is not Standard English (which itself grew out of a dialect) that has somehow gone wrong.

Direct and indirect speech

Direct speech is the reporting of what someone has said or written by quoting his/her exact words. Indirect speech tries to get over, or convey, what was meant, without repeating the exact words.

Enjamb(e)ment

Sometimes known as 'run-on lines', enjambement describes lines of poetry in which the sense continues from one line to the next without a clear break. There are frequent examples of enjambement in the AQA *Anthology*, for example the opening of 'This Room' (page 14):

> This room is breaking out
> of itself, cracking through
> its own walls

Enjambement generates two sets of meaning:
1 the grammatical sense of the complete sentence
2 the sense created by each individual line
In 'Vultures' (AQA *Anthology*, page 10), for example, there is continuous enjambement and the first sentence is not completed until line 13. Notice how the poem's line structure gives unexpected prominence to certain words, e.g. 'broken', 'affectionately'.

Evaluation

Looking at a text and considering its value or worth. When you are asked to evaluate the effectiveness of a piece of writing you must consider the impact the piece might have on the reader.

Flier

A short piece of printed material that is widely distributed.

Font

A full set of printing type or screen characters of the same design, e.g. Times New Roman, Arial.

Genre

A type or form with identifiable characteristics. In writing this could mean a leaflet, a letter, an article etc. In film, genre could refer to horror films, action adventures etc.

Hyperbole

Deliberate exaggeration for effect. Hyperbole is widely used in advertising, e.g. 'the *ultimate* garden hose'.

Imagery

Descriptive language in a work of literature that appeals to the senses.

Integrated comment

A quotation or reference that forms part of a sentence (often by being placed, or embedded, in it) and is not on a separate line.

Interpretations

Different ways of reading and explaining a text. Texts often have more than one interpretation. For example, 'The Song of the Old Mother' in the AQA *Anthology* (page 46) can be interpreted as a poem about responsibility, or lazy youth versus the hard-working mother.

Juxtaposition

Placing two or more words/phrases/images etc. side be side for (ironic) contrast. For example, in the *Anthology* poem 'Vultures' (page 10) the reference to 'human roast' is placed near that to 'a chocolate' for the commandant's child.

Kicker

A newspaper or magazine story designed to stand out from the rest of the page.

Layout

The general appearance and design of the text and images on a page.

Line grammar

The way in which lines of poetry divide up the sense of what is said. Poetry is written in lines that might not always correspond with the usual grammatical sense. The opening and closing words of a line tend to be particularly important because they stand out and attract the reader's attention.

Literal meaning

The word-for-word meaning, which takes no account of implied or wider meanings. For example, 'The bed is lifting out of its nightmares' cannot literally be true, so the poet must be suggesting something entirely different. You usually have to look beyond the literal meaning of the words on the page.

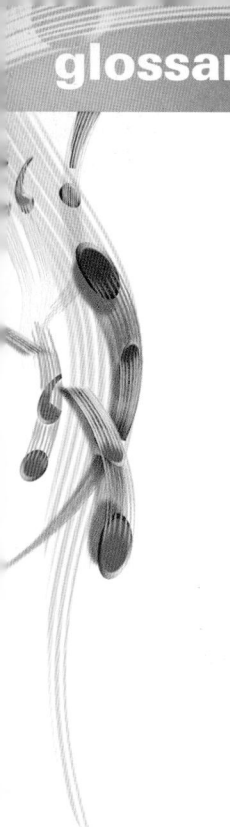

Beware of using 'literally' simply to give emphasis. Don't say 'I was literally drowned on the way to school this morning' when you really mean you got very wet.

Logo
A design used by an organisation that acts like an emblem.

Mark band
A group of marks that cover the top and bottom of a grade on an examination paper.

Mark scheme
The document examiners use to mark candidates' scripts to the same standard.

Media
Any means of mass communication, including film, newspapers, adverts etc.

Media terminology
The words used to describe the features of media texts.

Metaphor and simile
Both these figures of speech use **comparisons** to make an idea more vivid. Metaphor and simile are often referred to as **imagery**.

Metaphor involves an **unstated** comparison and is a natural part of our language. We use metaphors all the time without really noticing, as in 'The footballer *smashed home* a goal' (obviously nothing is actually smashed).

Simile involves a more **direct** comparison and is identified by the use of 'like' or 'as'. Like metaphors, similes are often used in everyday speech, e.g. 'The class rushed *like a herd of elephants.*'

Shakespeare's 'Sonnet 130' (AQA *Anthology*, page 50) mocks the exaggerated and fanciful imagery contemporary poets often used to praise their mistress:

> My mistress' eyes are nothing like the sun;
> Coral is far more red than her lips' red.

Non-fiction
Writing consisting of factual information and ideas.

Onomatopoeia
Words that imitate the sound being described, e.g. 'crackle', 'moan', 'sizzle'. Writers certainly attempt onomatopoeic effects, as in Tennyson's reference to 'The murmuring of innumerable bees', but you should be careful not to think that every use of a word connected with sound is an example of onomatopoeia. Besides, few words actually imitate a sound.

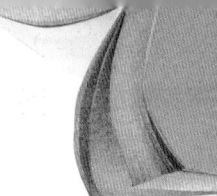

Organisational devices

Features such as paragraphs and columns.

Paraphrasing

Restating something in your own words.

Participles

Participles are forms of verbs and are made in two ways from a basic verb. There are two types of participle — **present** and **past**:

Verb: shout
Present participle: shouting
Past participle: shouted

The present participle can suggest continuous action and, skilfully used, can build up a sense of excitement. For example, 'This Room' (AQA *Anthology*, page 14) and 'Patrolling Barnegat' (AQA *Anthology*, page 49) both make use of this effect.

Persuading

Trying to make someone think or do something.

Point of view

This term has two senses:

1 an opinion on a subject or an attitude towards something — usually in contrast with another opinion
2 the position of a narrator; e.g. 'My Last Duchess' is written by Browning but the tale is told from the point of view of the Duke of Ferrara

In English Paper 1 you are required to compare and contrast pieces on the same subject written from different points of view.

Presentational devices

Visual features, such as bullet points, bold, italics, that are used to make writing more accessible to the reader.

Purpose

Why a particular text has been written in the first place.

Repetition

Repetition occurs in all kinds of writing. It can take a number of forms and has various effects. Most obviously, it can be used for **emphasis**, but it may also establish a **pattern**, as in the repeated stanza form of 'Not My Business' (AQA *Anthology*, page 15). Sometimes it can create an almost hypnotic effect, as in 'Limbo' (page 5).

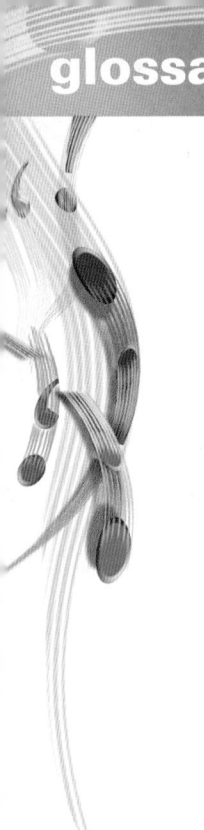

Rhetorical question

A question that presumes only one response, so it does not require an answer. Rhetorical questions can be used as a means of drawing your audience in and getting it on your side, e.g. 'Who could refuse someone who has been through such a terrible ordeal?'

Rhyme

Rhyme is probably the most familiar feature of poetry, although not all poetry uses rhyme.

The most common type is **end-rhyme**, in which the last words in lines of poetry have matching sounds, but rhymes can also occur within lines. Poems often have distinctive **rhyme schemes**, so that there is a regular pattern of rhyming syllables. There are innumerable possible rhyming patterns, and some specific forms of poetry, such as the **sonnet**, have strict rhyme schemes.

Rhyme can capture our attention in ways that stretch beyond the basic meaning of the words. For the purpose of the examination, it is useful to think about the meaning and force of the words that the rhymes draw to your attention.

Rhythm

Read out *any* sentence in English and you will see that there is a reasonably regular pattern of stressed and unstressed syllables. Although it depends on exactly how you say it, the stress pattern of the opening line of Joyce Cary's 'Growing Up' (AQA *Anthology*, pages 73–77) looks something like this:

Rob**ert Quick**, com**ing home af**ter a **bus**iness trip, **found** a **note** from his **wife**.

Poets organise stresses into conscious patterns. There is a large number of terms for rhythmical patterns in poetry, all with Greek names. The two most common patterns reflect the basic stress patterns of ordinary speech:

❊ **iambic**: unstressed followed by stressed (~ /) as in ex**am**
❊ **trochaic**: stressed followed by unstressed (/ ~) as in **Eng**lish

In traditional poetry it is often easy to recognise a regular pattern of stresses. Take this example from 'Tichborne's Elegy' (AQA *Anthology*, page 48):

~   /   ~   /   ~   /   ~   /   ~   /
My prime of youth is but a frost of cares

Much modern poetry uses a more flexible approach, often closer to natural speech, and the rhythm is more of a pulse than a regular pattern. A good example is 'Two Scavengers in a Truck…' (AQA *Anthology*, page 8).

For the purpose of the examination it is best to concentrate on spotting the **main** stresses, especially where they strongly emphasise the sense, as in

Brathwaite's 'Limbo' (AQA *Anthology*, page 5) or Walt Whitman's 'Patrolling Barnegat' (page 49).

Setting
The place or situation that forms the background to a piece of narrative. This might give you clues as to the wider meaning of the text.

Sonnet
A sonnet is a poem of 14 lines with a strict pattern of rhyme and rhythm. For the reader, the rules are less important than the way the ideas are set out. There are slightly different forms of sonnet but they share a similar **concentrated** three-part thought structure:

1 key idea
2 development
3 conclusion, often with a twist or sting in the tail

Standard English
Standard English is difficult to define, but it is the English you would associate with 'educated' speakers and expect to find in newspapers, textbooks, business documents and so on. It is extremely varied, however, and although you may find large differences in the language of the *Sun* compared with *The Times*, for example, they are both written in Standard English.

Standfirst
The introductory paragraph before the start of a feature in a newspaper or magazine.

Sub-heading
A heading less important than and 'under' the main one.

Symbol(ism)
A symbol is an object, person or event that represents something more than itself. For example, red has come to symbolise danger.

   Writers often employ symbolism but it is up to the reader to make the connections, which may be suggestive and vague. Successful use of symbolism should stimulate our imagination and prompt us to think beyond the text's immediate subject matter. Many of the texts in the AQA *Anthology*, such as 'This Room', 'Vultures', 'Flight' and 'Snowdrops', have strong elements of symbolism.

Tone
The kind of voice in which something is written (sarcastic, light-hearted, depressing etc.). The tone of a piece of writing is closely linked to its mood.

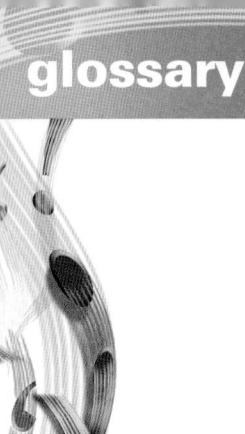

Verbs

Words such as 'run', 'talk', 'investigate', 'consider' and 'sing' are all verbs. A verb is essential to form a sentence; it is the one word that cannot be left out. For example, 'The student two gallons a day' does not make sense.

You will come across **minor sentences** that do not contain complete verbs. They are often used in newspaper headlines such as 'MOTORWAY TRAFFIC CHAOS FURY', and writers sometimes use minor sentences for special effect. Walt Whitman's 'Patrolling Barnegat' (AQA *Anthology*, page 49) is one long minor sentence, because apart from the words placed in brackets it uses incomplete verbs: 'the sea high running' rather than 'the sea is high running'.

Word art

Unusual lettering that is designed to make parts of the text stand out.